CHRISTIAN KUNDALINI SCIENCE: PROOF OF THE SOUL- CRYPTOGRAM SOLUTION OF EGYPTIAN STELA 55001- & OPENING THE HOOD OF RA

CHRISTIAN KUNDALINI SCIENCE:

PROOF OF THE SOUL-

CRYPTOGRAM SOLUTION OF

EGYPTIAN STELA 55001-
&
OPENING THE HOOD OF RA

BY THE KNOWLEDGE OF HE WHO HATH
OPENED THE PATH OF THE BRAZEN SERPENT

To help strengthen The Christians,

To inform those whom are listening

BY FRANK M. CONAWAY, JR.

ISBN 978-0-578-10079-1

ISBN 978-0-578-10079-1

CONTENTS

MASTER 55001 # 9

Concept: Meta Chronicles "Cipher of Rev 13.18"

An answer to the 666 riddle and The Turin Erotic Papyrus Stela 55001!

ETA - PHI - RHO - ETA - NU =

8 + 500 + 100 + 8 + 50 = 666

Master Works of Ancient Art from the British Museum "Eternal Egypt" and "Turin Stela" 55001

FIRST PAGE

Romans 1:14	I am debtor both to the Greeks, and to the Barbarians; both to the wise, and to the unwise.
Romans 1:15	So, as much as in me is, I am ready to preach the gospel to you that are at Rome also.
Romans 1:16	For I am not ashamed of the gospel of Christ: for it is the power of God unto salvation to every one that believeth; to the Jew first, and also to the Greek.
Romans 1:17	For therein is the righteousness of God revealed from faith to faith: as it is written, The just shall live by faith.
Romans 1:18	For the wrath of God is revealed from heaven against all ungodliness and unrighteousness of men, who hold the truth in unrighteousness;
Romans 1:19	Because that which may be known of God is manifest in them; for God hath shewed [it] unto them.
Romans 1:20	For the invisible things of him from the creation of the world are clearly seen, being understood by the things that are made, [even] his eternal power and Godhead; so that they are without excuse:
Romans 1:21	Because that, when they knew God, they glorified [him] not as God, neither were thankful; but became vain in their imaginations, and their foolish heart was darkened.
Romans 1:22	Professing themselves to be wise, they became fools,
Romans 1:23	And changed the glory of the uncorruptible God into an image made like to corruptible man, and to birds, and fourfooted beasts, and creeping things.

Ezekiel 39:24	According to their uncleanness and according to their transgressions have I done unto them, and hid my face from them.
Ezekiel 39:28	Then shall they know that I [am] the LORD their God, which caused them to be led into captivity among the heathen: but I have gathered them unto their own land, and have left none of them any more there.

"SEE THE HAND, SEE THE NAIL"

This is a message ciphered from the ideogram of the tetragramation as given on YouTube: "The Secret Name of God" at http://www.youtube.com/watch?v=1wiBtYITrxM.

On the YouTube video, the speaker says that Moses was told, "I will be as I will be". "The Secret Name of God" at http://www.youtube.com/watch?vCHBGgU9IPwc. You might want to look at this: "The Secret Name of Jesus" at http://www.youtube.com/watch?v=LBdfYNK_lvM&feature=related.

I AM THE LORD

In the book, *Math for Mystics* on page 62, there is figure 5-24 Hebrew Gematria Chart. What I would like to discuss here is the gematria of the Tetragrammaton. The Tetragrammaton is comprised of three letters and one letter twice. The letter sequence is "Yod Heh Vav Heh". You see earlier where this was ciphered to say "See the hand, see the nail". I do not think that this is the total cipher. Let me go step by step. Step one: "Yod Heh Vav Heh" equals to "hand window 'doorknob or nail'. The number values are 10, 5, 6, and 5 which totals 26. 26 could be ciphered as 20 plus 6. Twenty is defined as "palm of the hand". Six is defined as "doorknob or nail". Let us return to the letter meanings: "hand, window, doorknob or nail", window. The hand opens the window, the hand opens the door by the doorknob, if the hand does not open the window or the door by the doorknob, the window or door is nailed shut. The key to what I am pointing out is the "or" of Vav.

ON THAT DAY

On that day when the land had come to an uprising, I was there to see it. Upon that day, their voices did irritate my ears. On the beginning of that time of the great change in the land, their faces were valid for me to turn from. On the nineteenth day of my youngest one's days, so did a "change" rise up in the land. And so I saw such a day, I looked and was amazed. I turned my face, heart, and ear to reading The Word about The Lord. I believe that I was a Christian in the day of change of this life.

In short, what The Bible is saying is that there are some negative spirits running around here!

THEY JUST CANNOT

They just cannot hear you. Calm down and listen to the answer that people give you. Listen to hear how people answer you. See if they answer what you ask. This might be right on time with "Let them who have an ear listen"!

Matthew 10:27 What I tell you in darkness, [that] speak ye in light: and what ye hear in the ear, [that] preach ye upon the housetops.

Revelation 1:8 I am Alpha and Omega, the beginning and the ending, saith the Almighty.

Revelation 2:7 He that hath an ear, let him hear what the Spirit saith unto the churches; To him that overcometh will I give to eat of the tree of life, which is in the midst of the paradise of God.

Revelation 2:11 He that hath an ear, let him hear what the Spirit saith unto the churches; He that overcometh shall not be hurt of the second death.

Revelation 2:17 He that hath an ear, let him hear what the Spirit saith unto the churches; To him that overcometh will I give to eat of the hidden manna, and will give him a white stone, and in the stone a new name written, which no man knoweth saving he that receiveth [it].

Revelation 13:9 If any man have an ear, let him hear.
Cite: http://www.blueletterbible.org

THE MISSING GLYPH

There is a symbol that can be found in New College Edition – The American Heritage Dictionary Of The English Language – 1976 shown for the term ankh. The caption says "illustration on 19th Dynasty Egyptian papyrus". It looks like the image of a man with a bird's head with a round ball on it sitting on a structure with a raised ankh coming out of its uplifted knee. The glyph is not listed in the rear content of illustrations on page 1492 (look joke).

On some of the carducess symbols there are wings on the central shaft. I would just like to cipher the image at this point. The image shows a man dressed in the cloth of the inner garment, spiritual or etheric body. The bird head means that he has completed the great work by raising the kundalini energy to the mind. The missing ankh feathers cleaned the mind to polarize the mind towards the spiritual resting place of choice. Hence, he sits seated upon the top of the pyramid. He achieved this feat by using the key of life, ankh power, or kundalini sexual tantra to do so. Hence, the circle upon his head is the root power energy glyph surrounded by the kundalini energy serpent. The bottom of the bird mask has three tassels which represent the threefold or triangle paths of the one whom knows, or of him that possesses the all seeing eye. "If thy eye be one", and to see the glory or mystical halo! The kundalini when raised up or cultivated through the sexual system carries the root chakra energy to the crown. This crown chakra is comprised of the ankhs lower bar going inside of the oval which becomes surrounded by the cross bar. Hence, the concept of the conception or rebirth of oneself. It may be related to the mythology of the mystical phoenix.

DEDICATION

First, I would like to thank The Lord for leaving me something to do. I am thankful for finding a meaning of this life for me. I am happy about myself. I am pleased to have learned what I have. I am happy to be in The Word of The Lord. I thank The Lord for not leaving me as he promised. I thank The Lord for giving me understanding so that I am at peace with that. I thank The Lord for letting me survive upon this path so far. I thank The Lord for giving me something to look forward to other than physical death. I thank The Lord for giving me things that I asked for that brought me sorrow in the end. I thank The Lord for letting me ride. I thank The Lord for all of His miracles. I thank The Lord. Thank you! Place your bets, last call! Yes, The Lord to win, betting "EVERYTHING". ALL IN!

Love,
Me

AN AUTHOR

I want to be very clear about one point. I am not an author. I am a scientific investigator. I might be called an etheric <eUtheric, eU = you, or e of you, energy you> scientist, baby! While we are on that, I know I am not using the rules of English grammar. You might call some of my sentences run ons. They are not. They a written in natural, ebonic <eubonic>, or mathematical comma splice subject based form. Also, I use <and> to inject sub thoughts. In addition, you might find a word spelled different ways. Check the spellings for stela on the web. I found three ways to spell it. Please forgive typos also. We'll get to them later. Thank you! I found something. I did not know what it was or represented. I had to publish a notice of finding to "clock" in my date of discovery like an academic patent Just think, if I found something and didn't know what it was, how could I start to explain what it was that I found?

OUR STORY

Our story begins on the worst day of my life. It was the worst day because what would happen would change the course of my life forever. It became the best day of my life because of the path that I was about to take. All was lost on this day. A radical change was about to take place. I was aware of this. What I did not know was that I was going to receive the command to "go back and read your bible immediately"! That was a double change. I was going one way, then I was sent in another direction. So, I went back and read the Bible in about fifty-six days as I remember it. When I was finished, I was more confused than before I had started. So much of what I had read for myself was in conflict with what I had been told.

There were concepts that were a part of my life, my ego, my mind set, that were not biblical. Let me make it clear for you without going into a dissertation on the subjects of which I can. What does a rabbit have to do with Easter? What does a cut down evergreen tree have to do with Christmas? Say, I never heard that the Lord of the Bible had come to Earth in a human form during the time of Sodom and Gomorrah. I did not know that there was a talking donkey like the Mr. Ed television show in the Bible. I began to look at this world in a different way. I wondered if someone, the world, was trying to put "the trick" on me! This is the old serpent and Eve scenario! I read the whole Bible. What did I learn! I was so confused about the whole text that I had to simplify that answer. I read that the beginning of wisdom was the "fear" of the Lord your God: Jobe 28:28, Pslams 111:10, Proverbs 1:7, 9:10, 15:33, Isaih 11:2 and 33.6! Nobody had said anything to me about "fearing" the Lord! Oh, I had heard in joking that the Lord would or could strike you down. I mean, that is such a rare thing that it is an ancient concept. Wrong! Oh, that is so wrong. That type of thought is not even biblical. That type of thought reaches out against what the Bible says within itself. That type of thought is stupid starting from the concept of "spare the rod and spoil the child" Proverbs 22:15, 23:13 and 29:15.

Anyway, I noticed the question at Revelation 13:18. I had no answer for it. I had looked up in the dictionary the term obelisk. I could not understand what was being described. At least I had a clue. And so, with these two questions, the quest began. Seeking the knowledge of the obelisk led me to so many things. One thing it did was lead me to the said lost knowledge of Egypt.

It was a very special day some years later. I had been studying the Bible stuff for some time. I had a cipher text for the Book of Revelation for years. I studied it as it related to the kundalini system to the Bible. I was clueless as to what one had to do with the other. Let me see how I can put this. The information about the kundalini system was intact and extensive. There were several systems that dealt with the kundalini knowledge. I would like to repeat this for a reason. The information about the kundalini system was intact and extensive. There were several systems that dealt with the kundalini knowledge. Think about this kundalini subject like this. Suppose you find a giant battleship in a dry dock in the middle of the desert. It has all the manuals to make it function. It still functions because the clocks still work. The automated systems are still on. You have the manuals, you have the contraption; but you have no idea as to what it does at its full capacity. You have all of these clues, but you do not know what it is when all of these things come together as one. Due to the cipher text, I focused on the meaning of the given answer to Revelation 13:18, the use of an obelisk, the design of The Great Pyramid, and the science of the kundalini.

On this special day, I was going to be honored for an unrelated achievement. I was getting ready for the event. It seemed that my research had come to an end. I had tried my best. I had been on the case like a saber tooth cat on a bone. I was satisfied with my effort. I was at peace with myself. I had gone all out to achieve the objective. “I had failed.” I had tried! Yeah right, loser. You are a sucker! Yeah, well I had tried so hard. I did the best that I could. It was kind of hurtful. Oh well. As I was getting ready for the event, I walked past a table with an Egyptian hieroglyphic book for children opened upon it. As I walked pass the book on the table, I looked at the hieroglyphics on the page. I walked past the table and said to myself what the hieroglyphics meant. I stopped because I had not remembered reading my definition. I went back to look at the given meaning of the hieroglyphics. Sure enough, my meaning was different than the book’s meaning. How could this be

I wondered? All I knew was that I was ciphering those hieroglyphics. I had stumbled upon the priesthood symbolic meanings or language. From there it was on to the grand experiment which I ciphered as being called “Opening the Hood of Ra”! This lead to the hidden science of the Ankh. This knowledge led to the ego based “one thousand strokes of the cinnabar techniques” which also could be called Kundalini Sexual Tantra.

Having said that, I would like to start with ciphering some of the Egyptian art work.

AUTHOR

They have this great collection of Egyptian art work. They say that they know that it has a meaning. They admit that they know not what it means. I do! They hid stela 55001 for over thirty years trying to decipher it. They admit that they know not what it means. I do!

RA'S TONGUE

In Egypt, the obelisks stand erect and point to the sky known as the cosmic canopy. Generally speaking, an obelisk is a marker for the position of a star, or used as a reference point in the science of surveying. This is also true of a pyramid. There are actual uses for those tools. The obelisk also has symbolic meanings. It should be noted that they are also called Cleopatra's needles. Here is where the symbology becomes somewhat dual in nature. On one hand, the tools symbolic nature could be related to sexual meanings. On the other hand, the symbolic meanings can be related to "the sacred priesthood arts". I would like to put it another way. Let us say you have a coin. The coin has two sides. One side is usually called heads, while the other side is called tails. The two sides are held together by the rim. The rim could be viewed as a serpent eating its own tail. How could the coin be ciphered from the Egyptian perspective? The head side of the coin could be called the Cleopatra's needle side. The tails side could relate to Osiris and his missing or hidden phallus or tail. So the Cleopatra side could be said to represent worldly ideas, while the Osiris side could represent the spiritual side of the coin. The Osiris side of the coin could be called the Dark Side. That side of the coin could be said to represent the lunar side. It is the side of the pitch dark night's sky. Just because the sky is dark, that does not mean that the moon is not out or above. What about the time during a solar eclipse? Is the moon out? Can you see the light of the solar prominences or coronal filaments? The question is, did anyone look inside of the green Osiris' pen head hat wearing mummy's mouth? There is something funny! Do you get it? The resurrected one's inner side. That might be a good hiding place for a symbolic ankh!

There is a way to look at this situation as a science. The two sides of the coin are a part of one coin. Therefore, the two are as one. You have the sun side and the hidden side with the rim at the same time. To put it another way, you have Adam, Eve, and the serpent represented all in one symbolic object, the Adam Kadmon coin so to speak. When one practices the yogi arts, the use of the tongue becomes part of the practice. As one learns about mantras, one begins to do tongue exercises. The tongue becomes an important part of the exercise. The tongue helps to make certain sounds. That is generally on the external level. On the internal level, the tongue's formation causes other sounds due to its formation during the inhalation process. This is the basic tongue training. The tongue could be thought of as a horizontal obelisk. That would be as the serpent that is not erect. You might even say symbolically it is a fallen obelisk. The first thing to do would be to cause the tongue to become erect. This symbolically relates to raising the obelisk. Once the tongue is raised, now the proper alignment must be found. The tongue must be seated or bridled. That place would be at the "hood of Ra", the rising star, or the Star Gate in the top of the mouth. It is like a baby chick breaking through its egg shell. This is symbolic of the Phoenix's mystical rebirth. The mouth is like a sea shell. Inside of the shell there is a muscle. That muscle feeds with a harpoon type of organ. It pierces <the side of> its prey and secretes a deadly venom.

Let me tie this altogether. The kundalini is said to lay dormant in the base root of the male's human spine. At this point, the kundalini serpent is as a discharged or uncharged snake. When the snake begins to gather charge, it begins to rise up the spine. It was first discharged during the first birth process called conception. This relates to the mysterious ankh symbol. As the kundalini recharges, so does the human body grow. The second discharge comes in the form of a nocturnal or sexual emission. This stage is called the world. The kundalini is like an electro-magnetic eel. It swims in the fluids of life. The third discharge is called the spiritual level. This is where the full charged kundalini serpent reaches the medulla oblongata and is blocked. The pulse reverses and its tail "speaks" with the forked serpent's tongue or teeth like those found on the bottom of the staff of Ra on the Wikipedia site. This reverse pulse sends electro-magnetic energy into the mystical tail like the legs on the said Congo snake. The useless legs become activated and open the hidden paths of Ida, pingala, and shushma. This puts three pressures on the Hood of Ra. This is symbolic of The Great Pyramid's symbology. In a way you could say that three hidden doors become pressurized at the same time. When the seals of the doors are compromised, the function of the serpent eating its own tail begins. This is where you have a rapid exchange of bodily fluid within one's own self. It could be said that the Nile has over flooded. This is the point where the seer or pharaoh is seated upon the grand chariot among the yin and yang Sphinx's of the Tarot card deck. This is part of the mystery. The second part of the mystery deals with this concept and the possibility of being able to impregnate a woman using the techniques of Opening The Hood of Ra. That is not discussed here because it is a part of Kundalini Sexual Tantra, the one thousand strokes of the chinabar techniques writings.

YOU'RE SO ESOTERIC

I am so esoteric. I am so esoteric you say. What? You mean that in 1492 when you thought that the earth was flat, I knew it was round. You mean that you are just calculating the speed of light, while its value is encoded in the measurements of The Great Pyramid of Giza! Now, let us just think about those two issues. No, you want to "come out of the gates", which means to criticize me for having a biblical understanding that you have never heard before? Why would somebody even try to tell you a thing? Look at how they came at me for trying to explain that "which they have no answer for"!

Imagine that, the type of person that says that another person is "way out in theory" because they have no theory. This is a very strange place. A place where one gets laughed at, and ridiculed for being smart. No, that is the dummies putting on the "I do not know sit" show. Laugh because it really is. Some people are so dumb that they do not even know that they are dumb. They think that they are very intelligent. Oh, do not let me fail to mention the second in the order. You see there are different levels of knowledge. Someone may be very proficient on one level and laughing at another students higher level failure. It is like a first grader laughing at a physics student wanting report card

QUICK PITCH

Request to suspend The Rules. Why? Timing can mean the difference of how the situation is handled. What rules to be suspended? Proper editing, headers, etc. Any Comments? Yes, when solving a question, it is important to “clock in” somehow first. In addition, a contract can be made in some unconditional ways. Request for “a favorable report”! Granted. I would like to call this “operation quick pitch”.

“TOPIC: MAN AS TWO CREATURES”

Once upon a time, long, long ago, I was given charge of a number of children. My instruction to them was to always do their best. That is what I expected from them. I would often lecture them on the subject of doing their best, working hard to reach a goal, and what to do if you slip. Now you can slip on your own, you might be pushed. Either way, one must get up after a fall. I also said that it was alright to cry. Sometimes crying might be good for you when you’re in pain. Now as far as getting up is concerned, I offered them two different philosophies. In the case of a general fall, I would suggest that they should “get up! Now in the case of being pushed, I suggest a different approach.

Step one is to realize that you have been torn down. Step two is to look into the laughing face or faces of them or them whom “tried” to take you down. Step three is to reach into your back pocket and get that emergency can of “whip ass” that I gave you. Step four is to open the can without spilling a drop. Step five is to raise the can of “whip ass” high into the air. Step six is to read the instructions that I wrote on the bottom of the can aloud. The instructions read: “But on that day!” Step seven was to pray to The Lord for help. Step eight was to pour the mystical I know I can "whip ass" right upon your own head. Step nine was "to get to working' as hard as you could. Also, remember to think often of their laughing faces. Remember how they laughed when they thought you were a loser. This was especially true for the academic arena.

Step ten was very important. Once you pour that liquid whip ass upon yourself and get to stepping; never, never, never ever look down. The reason is because once you start moving at speed, the ground below your feet might be bursting into flames. Step eleven was knowing that you could fail if you tried your best and that would be alright; but under no conditions may you quit. Quitting is not an option. Remember those laughing faces, often those are now your sworn enemies. This is the last step. Once you are finished your run, do not forget to look into the face of your enemies. You did well; you gave it your best shot. The End. Oh, I am so sorry I forgot to tell you the last part of the last step. After you look your enemy in the face, give quiet thanks for the negative fuel they gave you.

WHAT I HAVE TO SAY

I did the best that I could. To some that was not good enough. Pop pop told and warned me about that. Yet, still I tried. I never gave up. Winners never quit, and quitters never win; that is a song. I tried to remember my objective when I felt sorry for myself. I tried to remember that I had chosen this for myself when I was taking a beat down. I tried to imagine the look on their faces when they found out "I was the winner"! Yes, that is who I wanted to be! Yes, just like I told my children. "Da da said, you have to scrap until you die!" I did not ask more of them than I asked of myself.

To LaCynda, Kelly, and Frank; your daddy loves you. It became a gutter war. I hope to see you on the right side on the other side. Read your Bible for yourself. Know The Lord for yourself. Beware of wolves in sheep clothing. Cipher the sixes. That is all I should say about that.

Clue: Two times six is twelve, or the other way around. Where is the other six? It would be in the first. Answer that and you might be able to see the birth of the two times, one day, the other night, which is called The Equinox, or to you, "how did I get here"?

It is what it is. And to my grandchildren and beyond, I saw you in my mind's eye; that might be the price one has to pay for, defending the blood line against a spiritual pack of wolves dressed like The Lamb. You little ones get with The Lord also. That is what I want to tell you from me. Haters are going to hate. That is their job. Don't they have to receive their earned rewards in the next life so read The Bible? The Lord does not lie! I am telling you so. You might be in a "field with many", but there can be one true master. Check it out for yourself. Watch your back. Do not worry; they will betray you face to face also! That is how it came to me, but I had made myself ready by calculating the matrix of possibilities not knowing which one would be the path that I was on. Now I know! You should know that when I was confronted by that thing, I was able to reply in truth that "I am a Christian"! Here is my proof.

Really, my first book which is written in cipher form for you and others was my end game. I had already clocked in on what I had done and <dissed and covered> discovered. I am a Christian. My Christian blood runs through your veins. You were conceived of the conception of my seed. On the day, at the moment of the first of my three of only conceived, unto this date, I made a pact even unto myself to change. I asked that I would be able to raise your children in the ways that might help take you away from being worldly, but unto the Ways of The Lord. With that, at that moment, I placed my seal with a great bite from my mouth into a tree of the world. In other words, I gave "my word"! I gave my word because I trusted no one else to teach you what I felt the truth was. This and I am the reason that at a very young age you all began to accelerate. You three have tasted the rewards of being the best of the best. I did that. I taught you. I drove you. It was me no matter what they say. Be respectful when you are able to see the truth. Be humble. You have nothing to do with it, so says me. Few even have a path of escape. Less have the ability, capability, or passion to even try. You three have that because I brought it out of you. You have my blood. I have taught you. With what I have left for you, and that which you saw and I taught; you can unfold unto yourselves. You do not even know what I taught you because I did not define what it was to you that I was teaching. You also have the power to reject what I say. To you whom are wise, I would suggest that you "test" it out first before you reject it. Oh, how long might it take? If I told you that, you might feel like I felt when I read about a martial system that I wanted to learn. The instructor answered "about twenty years"! I thought to myself, "that would make me thirty-six"! I then closed the book, only to get to start training.

To El L, Kel El, and Mister Jiggie, "get to working out'! Grandmaster Butcher told me 'there ain't no <it a song> stopping us now, we are on the move". Sorry for the time we missed. A man has to do what a man has to do. Get it on. Love Dada and Pop pop Frank M. Conaway, Jr., or whatever you call me.

P.S. If you should ever "hear" from Metatron, tell him I said hi and do not seek to become infinite like the term pi. Hay, I made it so far, and they call me by another name. They call me Mister Delegate, Blessed be His Name! Be in this world, but not of it. Be Spiritual!

WIKIPEDIA ON THESE

5449 Pyramid

666

Adam Kadmon

Adam Rutherford

Adam Rutherford Pyramidology

Adze tool

Alembic <= mukluk>

Akhet

Akhet Khufu

Amen

Amphora

Amun-Ra

Amon-Re

Amoun

Ancient Egyptian Religion

Animal worship

Ankh

Ankhesenamun

Anthropomorphis

Anubis <= Kundalini guide with hook for the mouth>

Aphelion

Armon Min

Bacchanalia

Bacchus (Leonardo)

Baphomet

Bar-shih

Belly Dance

Bes

Bethlehem Line

Binaural

Bolt of Brahma NADI

Book of the Dead

Bottony

Brazen Serpent <= KUNDALINI>

Caduceus

Cardinal direction

Cartouche

Celestial Mechanics

Centaur

Chakra, etc

CHI KUNG

Chebar

Chimera – Kundalini

Christopher Columbus

Chronology of the Bible

Classical element

Cleopatra's Needle

Coffin texts

Comma splices

Congo snake

Cross

Crux

Cynocephaly

Decipherment of Egyptian Hieroglyphs

Deir

Deir el Medina

Dendera zodiac

Denderah

Djed

Dubhe

Eghptian

Egyptian Pantheon

Egyptian soul

El-Medina

Elohim

Entity

Eroticism

Etheric <most times shown in a female form <et her I <see> light>

Event horizon

Face on Mars

Fibonacci

First Balkan War

Frankenfish

Funerary text

Golden Mean Ratio

Granodiorite

Griffin

Hale Boop

Hathor

Hatshepsut

Hieroglyph

History of Muslim Egypt <639 A.D. – 1517>

Hybrid

Ichthys

Icosahedron

Immutable Seed

INRI

Isis

Jackal

Jacobson's Organ

Joseph Smith Papyri

Kabbalah

Kama Sutra

Karate

Khufu Ship <PYR>

King Cobra

King Scorpion

King Snake

Kinsem Institute

Kundalini <CHECK NUMBER OF SITES ON THE WEB>

Kundalini syndrome

Kung Fu

Landscape Zodiac

Lexigram

Life-death-rebirth deity

List of Ancient Egyptian Papyri

Man in the moon

Manteia

Mantra

Mart

Mathematical Constant

Matrix <also means womb>

Mekubbalim

Merkebah <The Ship>

Metaphysics

Metatron

Min

Minotaur

Moses

Muslim conquest of Egypt

Mystical coffer

Nacheshim

Nacheshim Seraphim

Nada

Naga people

Nagas

Narmer

Narmer Palette

Nebamun

Nehushtan

Nemes headdress

Obelisk

Opening the mouth ceremony

Ophiuchus

Osiris

Ostrica

Patriarchal cross

Perihlion

Phallus

Phoenix

Phren

Phrenology

Pope Theophilus of Alexandria

Pyramid Inch

Pyramidology

RA

Ramesses

Rosetta Stone

Samadhi

Satanic Cross

Sefirot

Senatus consultum de Bacchanalibus

Senenmut

Sephirothic tree

Serapis

Set Maat

Seti

Sexual Zodiac

Sistrum

Sothic cycle

Spermo-gnostic

Sphinx

Standing columnar wave

Star Tetrahedron

Stela <also seen spelled as Stelae, Stella, Stele>

Sushamna

TAI CHI

Tantra

Tar Socar

Tasmanian Devil

Temple of Abydos

Temple of the Stars

Tesla

Tetrahedron

The Four Sephirothic Trees

The Going Forth of Wadjet

Theriocephaly

The Sphenoid Bone

Tree of Life

Trefoil

Trinity

Turin Erotic Papyrus <1150 B.C.E.>

Tyet <Ankh Book>

Unveiling

Uraeus

Virility

Wadjet

Widget

Yerkish

Yoda

Yoga

Zodiac

Zohar

Zoomorphism

ME

Some things you are going to have to do for yourself for yourself. You need to define exactly what it is that you need. I am sorry if my train does not go your way. Check this out. If you know you need to lose weight, hey, when someone calls you to come help bake cakes, you are busy. Tell them that you can hear your mother calling you. Tell them that your dog is barking. Me, I have got to go down to O'dells night club. What, after I get to know you for two years or more, it will be great. Oh yeah, I have got to go down to O'dells.

I am very busy. You ask "doing what"? Doing me. In the meantime, I have got to go down to O'dells. Hey, hey, hey; you do you. I have got to go down to O'dells. You do what you all old people do, and I will do me. It is like Denzel Washington said in the movie "Mo Better Blues", "I want to love you for the rest of my life, tonight"! After that is what that woman said about being an adult in the airplane movie about the miles traveled. I think "Up In The Air". That is what I am talking about. Check this out: "How are you doing tonight!" What kind of time are you on, today!"

GONNA

I was going to hold this back to the end, but naw; on April 7, 2010, that is not my style. The way I do it is to just let you have it. Gotta go all out, baby! So with that, I am coming in hot with a full load! We are going into Lamborghini territory.

MIND RIGHT

You can get it if you want it, but at the first sign of that drama you have got to go! Be happy that you go, because you can go and get your mind right. Now, if you get your mind right, you might be able to come back. But if I have to go, I am gone! And as far as that "how do you like me now" thing goes, it is only like that because you did not know me then!

DIDN'T SAY

Are you willing to go into "The Pits of Hell" to fight for this woman? Woo, woo, woo; didn't anybody say anything like that to me about "this"! Well, if the two <of you> become as one, if she falls, won't you have to "go down" to pick her up? Nah, didn't nobody say nothing to me about nothing like that there. "Thou shall not fornicate". Why, is this an ungodly woman? Don't you want to become as one? I don't know about all of that!

It came upon me in the convenience store, why I am having many <women> problems. I am a Christian. I ask <require> them to read the Bible from "cover to cover". Suddenly, they have problems. It's not them; it's me, for I am a Christian. "So as a Man think; so is He"!

MY RAP

If they won't do it for themselves and or The Lord, they won't do it for you – dummy! Oh, The World! You are trying to convert The World, how silly!

ATTRACTED

Sure they are attracted because they "want to come into the light". Pass not. They "desire" what they don't want!

THE COST

Sometimes I forget why some of the things happen in my life. Sometimes I lose very close friends due to my own final objective.

Every so often I feel a little sorry for myself. I knew the cost, but I hoped that it would not come to these things. I was often shocked at the way some situations unfolded. In some cases, I could see the events unfolding long before they did. I often asked myself why must some of these things happen. I already knew the answer. In a great number of cases, the problem in the equation was me and my objectives. I was on the academic field of battle. I was running with the ball. I was moving very fast. Sometimes I could feel the intensity with which I was moving. It seemed as if I was on fire with clear flame. I had done it before. As a matter of fact, two times often come to mind. One of the times was when I had achieved the highest average of my high school's junior class. At that time, I had no idea as to what I was doing. The second time was when I won first place in mens heavy weight white belt division at a karate tournament. This was a huge tournament. I think of it as the last battle of the Karate Wars in Maryland. When the dust cleared, I was the last man standing. Again, I knew not what I had done. I had become the best of the best. I had done the work. I had put in the time. In the end there was one. That one was me. I am going for it one more time. I feel that I have paid the price. With that, I go for it again. I feel that the next subject is due its own chapter because of the high value to me of what they did.

HOPE FROM KNOX

What can I tell you about a person called "Knox"? I had often felt sorry for myself because of my loss. Sometimes I would feel really down about the situation.

As fast as Knox had come, Knox had gone away. Then Knox was no more. Here comes my Swag! In the worst of it, I would recall who I was. I would recall that I was on the field of battle. I would recall as to what my objective was. Knox knew this. Knox new this. Here I go Knox, thanks for the help on the 55001 tip.

THE PLACE

Where is the promised land for me? It is a place where I can choose where I want to go in the next life. The promised land is a place where I can decide for myself if there is an afterlife. The promised land for me is a place where I can learn freely about my philosophical belief system. The promised land for me is a place where mental ability can determine who I am whether other people can accept it or not. The promised land for me is a place where I can be laughed at because of knowledge. The promised land for me is a place where I can have hope that some of all the people I have ever meet won't be going my way.

In my promised land, they who knew me, but did not know me, won't know me until I get where I am going! Now, that is the promised land for me. A place where I can bet upon myself – to win!

FUNNY 666

<3/22/10> Suddenly it came to me, not only are the seals covered by riddles, but the answer to Revelation 13:18 is covered with seals. Watch this. First, one must read the book to even realize that the question exists. Second, one must go upon the quest to find the answer. Third, one must ponder what the answer and question may mean. Fourth, one must try to figure out what do you do with the answer that you calculated. Fifth, once you figure out what you can do with the answer, you have to figure out how you are going to try to do whatever it is that may be the result of doing what is implied. Sixth, now you have to do it, whatever it is. Seventh, if you were able to do all of that, and if you were successful; now you need to figure out what it all meant. Now that is funny!

CAN'T FORGET

Just wanted to say thanks to Nakamichi aka Knox. Also, thanks for that paper work with that date and the comedy stand up blue2orange jams.

I INTEND

With my writings, I intend to do a number of things. Mostly, "SHOW" that I could answer questions that many of 'the experts" could not. I intend to bring the sweet smell of victory to my friends, and the greatly agonizing violently academic devoid defeat to certain so called players. You need to mind your <yo> business, but since you did not: "Welcome into my world!" P.S. The look on your face, though I might never see it: Priceless! Hope to get my bookstore up and running at unseenbooks.com

I was thinking hard about coming forward with the answer to the question at Revelation 13:18. I have done a lot of work and writing. I have been waiting and working on this for years. Having said that, if I was in college, my last paper should be my best. So an answer to the 666 riddle is he-phern in the Greek. The number value is 8+500+100+8+50=666. I have had this information for years. This is why I used the term "Gnostic" in the title of my cipher book called *Baptist Gnostic Christian Eubonic Kundalinion Spiritual Ki Do Hermeneutic Metaphysics*, ISBN #0595206780.

Now a quick internet check shows this answer but does not go into detail as to what it means. I once read that a scientist said "yes gentlemen we have proven 'it' to be true, but we do not know what 'it is'!" It is this second "it" that I am writing about. There are a few things I want to say before I come on with it. On the internet, I find that the book of source is authored by James Morgan Pryse. The name of the book is The Apocalypse unsealed. What I feel that is not being spoken on is what group did Mr. Pryse belong to. He belonged to a gnostic group. Some acknowledgment should be given to Helena Petrovna Blavatski. She is the author of Secret Doctrine and Isis Unveiled. I feel that she should be acknowledged for her part in this puzzle unwrapping. As a side note, when I published my cipher book, *Baptist Gnostic Christian Eubonic Kundalinion Spiritual Ki Do Hermeneutic Metaphysics*, I was accused of being "agnostic". I tried to explain to this certain person that gnostic starts with letter g, while the term agnostic starts with the letter a. This explanation was not good enough for this gabber mouth. There is more that I could say about this traitor, but I will not! I then told them that I had to give credit to the gnostic group because I had gotten a "key" from them as an author. To no avail, gabby was not hearing it. How sad, so ignorant. While I am talking about these types of bogus comments, there was one person whom with laughter made an off comment. Where I come from, this is called "a crack"! This is what they said: "I know you feel bad about your book not making the New York Best Sellers List". I had to light all up into that person with their mind of a merkfish.

The purpose of my book, *Baptist Gnostic Christian Eubonic Kundalinion Spiritual Ki Do Hermeneutic Metaphysics*, ISBN 0595206786, was to "clock in" my discovery. What that means is that when you are a scientist, you have to make a published statement of find to receive credit. If you discover something, but you do not know "what 'it' is", you need to publish for your future credit. If at a later date someone else defines what you found, you get credit for "clocking 'it' in"! So my cipher text *Baptist Gnostic Christian Eubonic Kundalinion Spiritual Ki Do Hermeneutic Metaphysics* is a clock in that I had found something, but I could not define what it was that I had found. I know that I had an experience, but what "it" was I did not know. I needed time to research the event.

With that, I shall move on to the answer of what he-phren means. From my information, I can see that it has something to do with the mind. There is a description of there being an upper and lower mind. So here we see there are two minds in this science. I submit that the two minds relate to knowledge. In fact, the source question at Revelation 13:18 states that the topic relates to wisdom and knowledge. To me this implies and states that the answer should bring the finder some type of wisdom and knowledge. What type of "knowing" could a person acquire that is not included in The Bible? What could this have to do with Egypt? Moses was in Egypt. Moses was at the transfiguration. Moses had the staff and his hand as signs for the people. I argue that the sign of his hand was related to his face did shine. I think his face did shine means his electro-magnetic force which could be called virility. The Bible says that when Moses died he had his virility in him. A statement was made that if you were bitten on the heel by a scorpion; raise the brazen serpent up the pole. Let's think about the scorpion concept. A scorpion has two claws and a stinger tail. In the kundalini yoga system this would imply a jump starter for that system. It would tie together Ida, Pangala, and Shushama while injecting an upward force that could lead to a comma. Could this reflect upon the tree(s) in the Garden of Eden? The seven days or lights of rotation being the Chakras? Since I brought up yoga, I should make a comment. As I understand it, the yogi <yogeee, as in yo gee, yo gi, as in yo karate man, a. k. a. squid low is Doctor Detroit <de t riot>> is trying to achieve enlightenment. What does that term mean?

If we cipher the word enlightenment, we can see "the action of inner light". What is this inner light? I would like to ask a question. What do you consider the highest miracle in The Bible? To me, it would be "the raising of the dead"! We know the Egyptians dealt with "the afterlife"! Stela 55001 deals with the secret knowledge of the "afterlife experience". I call this sacred ritual when done on purpose "Opening The Hood of RA". It could be done three ways that I know of. The first way is by oneself using meditation. The second way is by using the union of a male and a woman. The third way could be with certain Egyptian "tools". The tools that I refer to are the ankh and that question mark looking device of Anubis. This becomes a strange play upon "a fisher of men". I have never heard of that before. I would talk about how you might use these tools, but that can wait until another time. Back to the question. You are aware that through the advances in medicine, many people have died and been brought back to life. Did they say anything about their "near death" experience? This type of knowledge was important to Pharaoh. Pharaoh would need to "know". This would give Pharaoh a very special position. Pharaoh would be a knower and not a believer. The knowledge is that trapped inside the flesh is the etheric body. During the ritual of Opening The Hood of RA, Pharaoh would see their "etheric body, other body, or ghost" during the phase I call the mystical coma. By knowing a truth about the reality of the next life, Pharaoh or The Seer would have an “inside clue”. Look at how Pharaoh is spelled. It could be ciphered as Ph-ar-aoh = Ph-ra-aoh = 6 second level + RA – Sun God <not Amenra or Raamen + aoh. What is wrong with “aoh’? Ah, you need daleth to move up and down the tree of knowledge. Daleth is the letter “d” on the first level. So? So, alpha “d” on the second level is “n”, as in Noah! How about a human “ark” or vessel? The meaning of Stela 55001 is graphically describing the sacred priesthood art used in the technique of “seeing the other self”. I should add that I found out that a stela is usually thought of as a tombstone! Some other time, on this topic.

PRICELESS

It is one thing to win, but there is something that is priceless. I may not ever see it. They who deserve it may never have it. I know if they knew that they would. They laugh and laughed at me when I said I could and would make it to the top of the mountain. Many who I met while on the path promised never to leave me. Not only did a great number leave me, but several set out to betray me. A few felt that my run was too hard for them. I understand that to a degree. I guess they have their own feelings about “The Reward”! But them whom left and betrayed me, they are the ones that I refer to here. I wonder if they will ask themselves “what does this mean”? “He won, oh no!” “Yah!” That look on their faces, now that is priceless!

INTRODUCTION TO STELA 55001

Sex in the Ancient World – Egyptian Erotica | Heritage Key Page 1 of 2

SEARCH

FAQ - SITE NEWS - ABOUT - CONTACT
REGISTER - LOGIN

Sex in the Ancient World – Egyptian Erotica

Sex in the Ancient World – Egyptian Erotica

by Wild-Dream Films

According to the producers of this documentary film, the sex lives of the ancient Egyptians have been 'hidden from history' for centuries: while some sexual images originating in ancient Egypt continue to be kept out of the public eye and are censored by authorities.

This programme about ancient Egyptian erotica takes a look at many of the aspects of sex in ancient Egypt through explorations of explicit graffiti and hieroglyphics, found on the walls of an ancient limestone tomb near the Valley of the Kings.

The film crew used computer graphics to re create one of the most famous Egypt erotic hieroglyphs - the Turin Erotic Papyrus, housed in the Museo Egizio in Turin.

The production crew travelled to Luxor, Deir el-Medina and Cairo to film Egypt's fascinating tomb's and temples in order to present the sexual mysteries of the symbols and images within their walls. The film claims to digitally recreate the 'first old men's magazine' and also to reveal what went on between the bedsheets in ancient Egypt.

History Channel (Sep 2009)
50 min

Reviews

World's Oldest Lads' Mag: Erotic Hieroglyphs Recreated For History Channel by Bija Knowles
"The producers of an upcoming film for the History Channel – Sex in the Ancient World - Egyptian Erotica – claim they've recreated the world's 'earliest pornography' - based on..." (read more)

Comments

Log in or Sign up to comment on and rate this item!

What do others think?

No comments have been left as yet.

Related publications **Related articles**

http://heritage-key.com/publication/sex-ancient-world-%E2%80%93-egyptian-erotica 4/6/2010

World's Oldest Lads' Mag: Erotic Hieroglyphs Recreated For History Channel | Heritage ... Page 1 of 2

SEARCH

Search

FAQ - SITE NEWS - ABOUT - CONTACT
REGISTER - LOGIN

World's Oldest Lads' Mag: Erotic Hieroglyphs Recreated For History Channel

Submitted by Bija Knowles on Fri, 10/16/2009 - 15:28

Review

Sex in the Ancient World – Egyptian Erotica

by Wild-Dream Films

History Channel (2009)

The producers of an upcoming film for the History Channel – *Sex in the Ancient World - Egyptian Erotica* – claim they've recreated the world's 'earliest pornography' - based on erotic Egyptian hieroglyphics.

The hieroglyphics in question, held in the Museo Egizio in Turin, are known as the Turin Erotic Papyrus and were discovered at Deir el-Medina near the Valley of the Kings. The parchments in question are fragmented, so the film production company used computer graphics to 'complete' the images and – in the words of Sion Hughes, head of business affairs at Wild Dream Films , 'recreate the world's first men's magazine'.

Hughes told Wales on Sunday : "In those days there was no television or newspapers, so the men who built the Pyramids had to make their own entertainment. And we were surprised to find that they were making the equivalent of 'top shelf' men's magazines in their spare time."

Wild Dream Films filmed in Cairo, Deir el-Medina, Luxor and Italy for several weeks and worked with several experts to examine what is known about the sex lives of Egyptians. The programme draws the conclusion that Egyptian society was discreet when it comes to sex – although apparently ancient Egyptians were far less embarrassed about it than we are today. Hughes adds: "We discover that very little has changed in 4,000 years. Despite man's advances in many areas of life and technology some things will always be the same and he still has an appetite for sexual images."

While the upcoming film for History Channel may well be the first to examine Egyptian attitudes to sex through the means of a TV programme, lots of research has already been done on the subject. A book published earlier this year - *Sex and Gender in*

http://heritage-key.com/review/worlds-oldest-lads-mag-erotic-hieroglyphs-recreated-history... 4/6/2010

Ancient Egypt. 'Don your wig for a joyful hour' edited by Carolyn Graves-Brown – brings together a collection of lectures given at a conference held at the University of Swansea, Wales, earlier this year. Some of the chapters of the book focus on the tomb of Niankhkhnum and Khnumhotep, the famous image that shows (possibly) two men kissing. A chapter by Jiri Janák and Hana Navrátilová takes a look at the Turin Erotic Papyrus, the Egyptian artefact examined and digitally created by Wild Dream Films.

Sex in the Ancient World – Egyptian Erotica is scheduled to be aired on the UK's History Channel at a date still to be confirmed.

About The Author

Bija Knowles

Last three pieces by this author: Lead Coffin Discovered in Gabii Contains Roman VIP | Heavy Rain in Rome Causes Major Damage to Domus Aurea and Trajan's Baths | Watch Restoration of Riace Bronzes Live and Online

Bija Knowles is a free lance journalist based outside Rome, Italy. She graduated in Italian and English Literature from the University of Birmingham, UK, and her main areas of interest are art, travel and history in Italy.

TRANSCRIPT OF STELA 55001 SHOW

<Credit is given to The History Channel and mReplay LiveDash is a registered trademark of mReplay Corporation. The information provided with Replay LiveDash is for informational purposes only. For more information, please see our terms of use. The network logos used on mReplay LiveDash are registered trademarks of those respective companies, including Fox, NBC, CBS, PBS, ABC, FX, TNT, ESPN, ESPN2, TBS, USA, MTV, VHI, Spike, A&E, Bravo, AMC, TLC, Animal Planet, ABC Family, Cartoon Network, Disney, CNN, CNBC, Fox News, MSNBC, Comedy Central, Entertainment, TV Land and Oxygen. These networks, Fox, NBC, CBS, PBS, ABC, FX, TNT, ESPS, ESPN2, TBS, USA, MTV, VHI, Spike, A&E, Bravo, AMC, TLB, Animal Planet, ABC Family, Cartoon Network, Disney, CNN, CNBC, Fox News, MSNBC, Comedy Central, Entertainment, TV Land and Oxygen are not affiliated with mReplay LiveDash, or mReplay Corporation.>

Sex in the Ancient World - Egypt
HISTP
Aired on Friday, Oct 23, 2009 (10/23/2009) at 02:02 AM
Like CUMMINS walls know life find Turin PARKINSON gods sexual NARRATOR Medina Egypt erotic important women Papyrus time love image Egyptians fertility images years lotus message kind picture This Egyptian young afterlife world lives site MANNICHE temple Dear BOOTH shows probably people view HUGHES papyrus having everyday today tomb women ancient sexuality scenes temples evidence must symbols music They Erotic

Transcript

00:00:00 outside Cairo, one item stands out.
00:00:04 Papyrus 55001– more commonly known as the Turin Erotic Papyrus.
00:00:13 >> DR. LISE MANNICHE: It's a very explicit sexual document from ancient Egypt.

00:00:18	It is a very rare example, because there aren't all that many of that kind.
00:00:22	>> NARRATOR: Depicted within its fragments are images of 12 ordinary men and women in explicit sexual positions.
00:00:29	For centuries, it was kept out of public view.
00:00:32	>> CHARLOTTE BOOTH: It was locked away in libraries and you had to go and register to look at it and have a very good reason for looking at it, and then it was only men.
00:00:40	So in Victorian times when it was published women would have no good reason to go and look at something as filthy as the Turin Papyrus.
00:00:48	>> NARRATOR: The controversy that has always followed the Turin Erotic Papyrus has created a mystery.
00:00:54	Even today, we don't know its true meaning.
00:00:57	Does it portray the sex lives of the gods and provide a coded message to the afterlife?
00:01:02	Is it part of an elaborate and mystical ritual of conception?
00:01:06	Or is it simply a relic of everyday erotica– an ancient pornographic magazine?
00:01:14	Now for the first time on television, we will decode this ancient puzzle.
00:01:20	By deciphering its images and symbols we will discover its true meaning and gain a more intimate view of the sexual lives of ancient Egyptians.
00:01:29	>> DR. RICHARD PARKINSON: By looking at the data we have for ancient Egyptian sexuality we get a sense of the people as they actually were, with the same issues, the same emotions, the same desires as us.
00:01:41	And I think that view of them is much more interesting than just seeing them as strange, exotic figures dominated by mummies, myths, magic and pyramids.

00:01:51 >> NARRATOR: For centuries, the sex lives of ancient Egypt were overshadowed by other civilizations.

00:01:56 >> HUGHES: The Greeks and the Romans have the reputation for being very lustful societies and that's partly because of the evidence that they've left behind.

00:02:05 We see orgiastic scenes on their dinner services or bestial action on tombstones.

00:02:11 >> NARRATOR: The full view of ancient Egypt was obscured.

00:02:15 >> HUGHES: The ancient Egyptians were a very sensuous, sensual society.

00:02:20 For an ancient Egyptian it was very, very important that you were an actively sexual creature.

00:02:27 >> NARRATOR: It was a cover-up aided by historians themselves.

00:02:31 Sexual artifacts recovered from ancient Egypt were often subject to censorship.

00:02:38 >> SCOTT: We have lost some of the sexuality from the ancient world.

00:02:41 In Italy, for example, the Popes decreed that all genitalia should be covered up with fig leaves.

00:02:46 And in the Victorian period, as well in the UK, this was not something which people wanted to see.

00:02:53 >> NARRATOR: One such example is the mutilated statue of Min, the Egyptian god of fertility, kept at the British Museum.

00:03:02 Significantly, the statue is missing one important item.

00:03:06 >> BOOTH: During the Victorian era the penis would be removed in order to save the blushes of people visiting the museum.

00:03:15 There's also another example of Armon Min but on a wall inscription.

00:03:20 >> NARRATOR: In this case, Min's penis could not be removed.

00:03:23 He had to be censored in a much more amusing way.

00:03:26 >> BOOTH: In the Petrie Museum the penis was covered up with the museum number, nicely put over it, again so that no one would actually see such a disgraceful thing in the public eye.

00:03:37 >> NARRATOR: Even today, some sexual images are kept hidden from the public.

00:03:41 Close to where the Turin Erotic Papyrus was discovered on the West Bank of Thebes, there is an archaeological site, 3,000 years old, kept secret from thousands of visitors nearby.

00:03:54 It contains one of the earliest slanderous pornographic images in history, and it remains concealed in a cave.

00:04:01 Not simply due to the nature of the image itself, but because of whom the image is thought to depict– Hatshepsut, one of ancient Egypt's few female rulers.

00:04:11 >> BOOTH: It's possible that it's the oldest piece of sexual graffiti in the world.

00:04:14 It's certainly not the oldest image of people having sex, but possibly the oldest piece of graffiti showing this kind of act.

00:04:23 >> NARRATOR: The drawing is located on the site of a temple in honor of the queen.

00:04:28 Creating such a sexually explicit image would have been dangerous for the artist.

00:04:33 >> LIZ CUMMINS: An image of the queen in a sexual position was a serious no-no for sure and would have been something that had to be hidden away, something that the person would probably get in serious trouble for if they were found out.

00:04:49 >> NARRATOR: Due to the controversial nature of this graffito, few academics have accessed the cave.

00:04:56 For this program we have been given permission to investigate this unique archaeological site.

00:05:07 >> CUMMINS: They block up the site to keep visitors out, and nobody gets to go in usually.

00:05:13 So now I'm getting to go in and I'm very excited, so we're going to take the door down and we're going to go in.

00:05:19 >> (speaking foreign language)>> CUMMINS: Wow, oh, wow.

00:05:31 This is... this is something.

00:05:35 >> NARRATOR: It is not known who cut the limestone cave, but it is thought to be one of the craftsmen from the Valley of the Kings who may have decided that it would be a good location for his own tomb.

00:05:47 For a number of years Liz has wanted to access this remote site.

00:05:53 >> CUMMINS: Wow, this is fantastic.

00:05:55 Oh yeah, I've only seen it in books and it's really good to see it in real life.

00:06:06 This graffito was probably created by one of the workers from around this area, so probably a tomb worker or even a temple worker.

00:06:15 >> BOOTH: The graffiti shows what appears to be Hatshepsut being taken from behind by who they think could be Senenmut, her steward and possible lover.

00:06:27 >> NARRATOR: Details of the drawing provide clues to its significance.

00:06:31 >> CUMMINS: You have the male behind a female, and it's believed that it might be Senenmut and Hatshepsut because we have here the headdress.

00:06:40 They think it's maybe the Nemes headdress which would have been a sign of royalty, and since it's obviously a female figure, they thought well, this was probably this was Hatshepsut.

00:06:50 >> NARRATOR: Why would someone take the enormous risk of portraying a royal figure in such explicit terms?

00:06:56 >> BOOTH: This was the artist's way of showing his distaste at the fact that they did have a female king– it went against the laws of Mart, it went against everything that Egypt stood for.

00:07:08 >> NARRATOR: The graffito offers a new view of the Turin Erotic Papyrus.

00:07:12 When matched against the Turin images, it shows similarities to one of the 12 sexual intercourse positions depicted.

00:07:19 Could it also have been a slanderous message?

00:07:22 The graffito does provide an uncensored glimpse of everyday life in ancient Egypt.

00:07:28 >> CUMMINS: It seems like it's a unique window into the world of the tomb workers that lived in this area and their concepts of sex in a completely different way than they were allowed to show in the temples and tombs.

00:07:41 Because they spent most of their time really showing things that only were part of this idea of decorum, and in here they could express themselves in a completely different way.

00:07:52 >> NARRATOR: But Egyptologists still face an incomplete picture of sexual life in ancient Egypt.

00:07:58 To get the full intimate details we must piece together the true meaning of the Turin Erotic Papyrus.

00:08:05 Could they be messages to the kings and queens of ancient Egypt?

00:08:09 Or perhaps to an even higher power?

00:08:12 To find out, we must explore the tombs and temples of the gods.

00:08:16 There, the walls are filled with hidden codes.

00:08:19 And if you know where to look, the sexual messages are everywhere.

00:12:15 >> NARRATOR: We are decoding an ancient sexual artifact known as the Turin Erotic Papyrus.

00:12:21 Could it be a message to Egyptian royalty, like this piece of graffito found near the Valley of the Kings?

00:12:27 Or could it be a message to a higher power?

00:12:30 A message to the gods?

00:12:31 To find out, we must enter the sacred temples– the gateway to the afterlife.

00:12:37 Here, the images contain a code– symbols filled with sexual messages.

00:12:42 >> PARKINSON: In religious iconography on temple walls you see a lot of gods with huge erections, you see deities having sex, but Egyptian temples are very much enclosed spaces which very few people would have access to.

00:12:55 >> NARRATOR: Journeying along the River Nile, a team of experts will enter the sacred heart of Egypt's most important temples.

00:13:02 By analyzing their artwork, they can unlock their hidden meaning.

00:13:07 >> SCOTT: In contrast to the showy pornographic world of ancient Rome, Egyptian sex is much more coded, much more symbolically displayed.

00:13:17 >> NARRATOR: Central to the tombs was the idea that when you died, your body would need to go to the afterlife.

00:13:23 The tombs were portals, and sex would be an important part of that transition.

00:13:28 >> BOOTH: When you die, the idea is it's not the end of life, it's the beginning of a new life, and the beginning of new life starts with birth.

00:13:35 So you do have the sexuality and fertility aspects associated with everything to do with death and the funerary rituals.

00:13:42 >> NARRATOR: Dr. Lise Manniche is one of the leading experts in the sexual history of ancient Egypt.

00:13:48 She has been studying Egyptian tomb art for the last 45 years.

00:13:52 >> MANNICHE: On the walls of some of the tomb chapels, we have a number of scenes that look like scenes out of daily life; the ideal daily life scenes: parties, banquets, etc.

00:14:03 But they all have a funerary purpose, because they are on the walls of a tomb chapel.

00:14:09 >> NARRATOR: The ancient Egyptians believed these images were instrumental in the act of being reborn.

00:14:15 >> MANNICHE: This is sex in disguise; you may call it like that.

00:14:19 It is a picture of the ideal occasion in real life.

00:14:23 In order to be reborn, you have to have these sexual activities that goes before any birth, birth or rebirth.

000:14:32 >> NARRATOR: Symbols that we see on the temple walls are also present on the Turin Erotic Papyrus.

00:14:39 >> MANNICHE: The key word here is the lotus flower.

00:14:41 The lotus flower is a symbol of resurrection.

00:14:44 Probably had narcotic properties, so it's not without reason that they're sniffing these lotus flowers, but they're just everywhere.

00:14:52 >> NARRATOR: There are also other similarities between the codes here and o mysterious papyrus, symbols that also ring true today.

00:15:00 >> MANNICHE: Sex is greatly facilitated, I think, the initial steps, by means of alcohol, and the Egyptians knew that, and we always have this triangle of sexuality, of music, and of drunkenness.

00:15:13 It really goes together.

00:15:14 It did then as it does today.

00:15:17 >> NARRATOR: The messages reveal that sex was central to rebirth in the afterlife, but their interpretation can be complex.

00:15:24 >> MANNICHE: Sexuality was of paramount importance, and it is displayed not directly, but through symbols.

00:15:24 >> MANNICHE: Sexuality was of paramount importance, and it is displayed not directly, but through symbols.

00:15:33 >> NARRATOR: Leaving the temples of Luxor behind, Lise is traveling to the Egyptian capital, Cairo, to study one of the most important finds from the ancient world: the treasures of Tutankhamen.

00:15:46 Hidden on a 3,500-year-old clothes chest, Lise believes she has found a significant clue to how the ancient Egyptians depicted sex in a covert manner.

00:15:59 >> MANNICHE: This is a clothes chest that was found in the tomb of Tutankhamen.

00:16:03 On it we see a picture of the king sitting on a chair shooting bow and arrow.

00:16:09 At his feet we have his wife Queen Ankhesenamun who's holding an arrow ready for him to shoot.

00:16:16 The mere fact that he's actually shown in that position shooting with bow and arrow takes us to the real significance of this scene, the symbolic, encoded message.

00:16:26 >> NARRATOR: The key to this clue is its double meaning.

00:16:29 >> MANNICHE: The word "seti" in Egyptian means "shooting," but it also means to ejaculate, which has very sexual significance because they wanted to be reborn in the hereafter, in the afterlife, and in order to be reborn, they had to have some sexual activity beforehand.

00:16:47 And this is what is explained here in a coded message.

00:16:51 And this is a way of visualizing this very vital sexual energy which they needed to be reborn.

00:16:58 >> NARRATOR: Hunting was a common metaphor for sexual prowess in the ancient world.

00:17:03 Similar codes have been found on the tomb wall of an accountant named Nebamun.

00:17:08 >> PARKINSON: It shows Nebamun accompanied by his wife, his young daughter, and he's out in the marshes hunting birds and catching fish.

00:17:16 And it is also, of course, an intensely erotic scene to the original audience's eyes.

00:17:23 >> NARRATOR: Traveling through the marshes is known to be an ancient Egyptian euphemism for having sex.

00:17:28 >> PARKINSON: All of these overtones of fertility, productivity, sensuality all combine in this image to suggest how Nebamun will be reborn in the eternal life, how he'll continue very much as a sexual, sensual being.

00:17:46 >> NARRATOR: Could the Turin Erotic Papyrus have been a link to the afterlife?

00:17:50 Could it have been a coded message to the gods?

00:17:54 >> MANNICHE: It does show the 12 positions of intercourse.

00:17:57 Whether they relate to this world or the next or to the world of the gods, that is very much debated at the moment.

00:18:05 >> NARRATOR: To find out, we must first explore the sex lives of the ancient Egyptian gods themselves.

00:18:14 >> CUMMINS: Only certain people would be able to come into this part of the temple, probably priests, not ordinary people who would be kept outside the temple precinct, so these images would be hidden and wouldn't be a part of what the everyday people would be seeing.

00:18:30 >> NARRATOR: Three hours south of Luxor is the temple of Abydos.

00:18:34 Hieroglyph symbols provide clues that sex was important to the ancient Egyptian gods.

00:18:40 >> DR. KELLY DIAMOND: The ancient Egyptians had two ways of writing their language, one of which was in hieroglyphics or sacred carved writings.

00:18:49 There's a lot of symbolic imagery behind both the illustrations themselves and the writing system, because each individual hieroglyph is, in fact, a picture of something.

00:18:59 There are a lot of different meanings, things can be read in a variety of different ways.

00:19:04 In this section right here, you can see this one particular sign, which is a phallus.

00:19:09 The phallus is part of the Egyptian repertoire of hieroglyphic signs and it can have one of many meanings, but it is indeed a very sexual symbol.

00:19:19 >> NARRATOR: The phallus hieroglyph signifies masculinity, aggression, fertility and sexual power, revealing a sexual side to the gods.

00:19:28 Sex was deeply ingrained into religious beliefs.

00:19:31 >> DR. KAREN EXELL: The whole of Egyptian society is certainly based around sex in the sense that they understood its importance and its significance; and that without the sexual act, their society wouldn't continue.

00:19:42 >> NARRATOR: Sex was also central to ancient Egyptian creation myths.

00:19:48 Contained within the British Museum is an ancient papyrus, which shows how the Egyptians believed their gods performed sexual acts to create the world.

00:19:57 It's a rare piece of evidence, which reveals that sex formed a magical and mystical aspect to religious beliefs in ancient Egypt.

00:20:07 >> PARKINSON: In one way, the Egyptians are very different from us: They are very discreet about human sexual activity, but when it comes to the gods, the iconography to us seems just to be simply pornographic.

00:20:20 >> NARRATOR: To represent how self-sustaining and fertile the Earth is, the ancient Egyptians show the auto-fellatio of the Earth god Geb.

00:20:29 >> PARKINSON: It's not something we would consider putting in a religious context; still less burying as a religious document with the priestess of the main god of the time.

00:20:39 >> NARRATOR: The men in the Turin Erotic Papyrus are all exceptionally endowed, like the god Geb.

00:20:45 Rather than mere mortals, could these men and their sexual acts be a depiction of gods in the afterlife?

00:20:52 To investigate further, we must go into the temples of Abydos.

00:20:57 Deep within its chambers is a phallic symbol linked to the story of Isis and Osiris; a mythical tale of life and rebirth.

00:21:05 >> CUMMINS: We're going into the chapel of Tar Socar and there's a few really interesting reliefs that are located here that show the god Osiris.

00:21:14 Here we have an image of the mummy form Osiris shown on a bed with the goddess Isis as a bird located on top of his erect phallus.

00:21:24 The scene is a lot more coded than you would see in a tomb or maybe even a graffiti or whatnot, because it shows the gods.

00:21:33 And so you don't have the image of Isis as a woman, you have an image of Isis shown as a kite or a bird of prey.

00:21:40 This was probably not a shocking image to the Egyptians, though.

00:21:45 It's something that does show the power of Osiris through his phallus, and it was very important to show these two on a different level, than say the rest of the divinities or even the rest of the population at large.

00:22:00 >> NARRATOR: Even today, this sexual artifact still holds a certain power for some visitors.

00:22:06 The site attracts women to the temples who are in search of the magic of the gods to help them.

00:22:11 >> CUMMINS: The phallus has been either chipped out, it's been touched.

00:22:16 Guardians come in, people come in and want to touch it and kind of be part of this power.

00:22:21 Even today, people go into temples and want to be part of this fertility that could even make them pregnant in modern-day times.

00:22:29 >> NARRATOR: So the coded symbols and graphic depictions were not just a way to be reborn into the afterlife.

00:22:35 They were linked to fertility in everyday life, and the act of sex itself.

00:26:52 >> NARRATOR: The Turin Erotic Papyrus offers a shocking-but- cryptic image of sex in ancient Egypt.

00:27:00 To understand its meaning, we are decoding other sexual images from the era.

00:27:04 They reveal that sexuality was connected with the gods and helped the transition into the afterlife.

00:27:12 But how did this affect ordinary Egyptians in their everyday lives?

00:27:16 >> EXELL: For the ancient Egyptians, sexuality was very much just a part of daily life.

00:27:21 From the few settlement sites that we have, we can see they lived in fairly small houses and would have lived on top of each other quite literally, so the sexual act would have been fairly visible to all the family.

00:27:32 >> NARRATOR: Sex, conception and fertility were closely linked with the gods– with one god in particular.

00:27:38 >> BOOTH: Bes is the god of fertility.

00:27:41 He is the protector of pregnant women.

00:27:44 He is the protector of young children.

00:27:47 >> NARRATOR: How did ordinary Egyptians, trying to conceive, interact with the god Bes?

00:27:52 A fascinating new site may provide intriguing answers.

00:27:56 It is situated 22 miles south of Cairo in Saqqara, which is also known as the City of the Dead.

00:28:04 >> MANNICHE: At Saqqara, there are the so-called Bes chambers, four little rooms decorated with figures of Bes and naked women on the walls.

00:28:14 >> NARRATOR: Mystery still surrounds this incubation, or Bes chamber.

00:28:19 >> SCOTT: These chambers seemed to have been used by people who were having trouble conceiving.

00:28:23 Perhaps they came there to sleep the night in the chamber and to go away expectantly hoping to conceive.

00:28:31 Perhaps they came to receive advice from the priests of the god himself.

00:28:36 >> NARRATOR: Bes is first and foremost a deity connected with everyday life.

00:28:40 He was considered to bring good luck and prosperity to married couples and their children.

00:28:46 He also played a vital role in the ritual of childbirth.

00:28:50 >> PARKINSON: Childbirth is always a dangerous time, and so various rites have to be performed and certain gods are really dedicated to watching over the new mother and the new child, such as Bes.

00:29:02 There's also a sense he's the household familiar.

00:29:04 He's a bit of a comic character.

00:29:10 >> NARRATOR: The mystical rites that surrounded Bes were also important in warding off evil spirits during childbirth.

00:29:18 In the Manchester Museum is a unique Bes mask, which may have been worn during childbirth by a priestess.

00:29:26 >> EXELL: This mask may have been worn by a dancer who would've been involved in a ritual, some kind of ritual dance to protect the household and protect the women.

00:29:33 >> NARRATOR: As well as ritual masks, priests would also use magic wands in the process of childbirth.

00:29:39 >> DR. JOYCE TYLDESLEY: They were used to maybe draw a circle, protective barrier around the mother and child.

00:29:44 Doing a ritual like encircling you to ward off evil and to keep goodness in might actually be a very comforting thing for the mother in labor.

00:29:53 >> NARRATOR: Bes is also believed to have a more erotic charge.

00:29:57 One theory suggests that he was used to prevent sexually- transmitted diseases.

00:30:03 A mural has been discovered which shows Bes tattooed on a young Egyptian woman.

00:30:09 Tattoos in Egyptian society were almost exclusively drawn on the most erotic parts of the female body.

00:30:16 >> BOOTH: What we've got here is a new kingdom fertility figurine.

00:30:20 She's got tattoos across her buttocks.

00:30:22 There's a line of dots rather like a belt, also a sign of fertility and sexuality.

00:30:29 Another interesting feature is the fact she doesn't have any feet.

00:30:34 And the reason for this is so that when she is placed into the tomb, she doesn't run away, taking her fertility with her.

00:30:40 >> NARRATOR: Egyptologists believe these statuettes, called “brides of the dead,” were symbols of fertility and rejuvenation.

00:30:47 Strange markings on tattooed mummies have lead other scholars to ask if tattoos were used to protect the unborn child.

00:30:54 One theory is that dots were tattooed on a woman's abdomen.

00:30:59 During childbirth, as the stomach expands, the dots would create a netlike structure, protecting the child.

00:31:06 But there is another side to the god Bes.

00:31:09 >> BOOTH: He's also the patron god of dancing, music, singing, getting drunk - all the sort of fun party aspects.

00:31:20 >> NARRATOR: Another depiction of Bes on the thigh of an Egyptian woman is shown on a blue bowl which dates to 1300 BC.

00:31:28 The woman depicted is a musician which is apt, as sex and music were very much linked.

00:31:34 Today, modern belly dancers use coin belts to accentuate the sensuality of the movements as well as the sounds.

00:31:42 And sound would be a key signifier of sex in ancient Egypt.

00:31:47 >> MANNICHE: There were also scenes of music, because music and sexuality go together.

00:31:54 >> NARRATOR: Images of music and dancing would signify another association with the gods.

00:31:58 One goddess in particular reveals another side to sex for the ordinary Egyptian.

00:32:04 The goddess known as Hathor, the daughter of the sun god Ra, was the most important deity in one's sexual life.

00:32:11 She was the goddess of physical love and spiritual love.

00:32:15 >> MANNICHE: There was one object that was particularly important in the cult of Hathor and that's what's called a sistrum, a sacred rattle, which has a picture of Hathor on it.

00:32:25 And whenever anybody rattled and made a noise with such a sistrum it meant that the goddess was present, she was there.

00:32:33 (rattling)>> NARRATOR: Could this sound have heralded a sexual act?

00:32:42 >> DIAMOND: We see in many tomb scenes, dating as far back as the Old Kingdom, where there are scantily-clad women who are dancing and shaking these sistra as part of a ritual celebration.

00:32:56 >> NARRATOR: The coded references on the temple walls between sex and music are mirrored on the Turin Erotic Papyrus.

00:33:03 Via our reconstruction, we have also discovered a sistrum on the papyrus, suggesting that the goddess Hathor is present in the sexual acts being carried out.

00:33:16 The gods and their rituals were seen to aid fertility and ultimately, the physical act of sex.

00:33:23 But how did ordinary ancient Egyptians feel about sex?

00:33:27 The Turin Erotic Papyrus provides a startling glimpse back 3,000 years. Through exploring the daily sex lives of ancient Egypt, can we unlock its graphic images?

00:34:33 >> NARRATOR: We know that some sexual images are connected with the gods...

00:37:48 and others with the rituals of fertility.

00:37:52 but could the Turin Erotic Papyrus have simply been ancient pornography?

00:37:56 To find out, we must first understand what the ordinary Egyptian considered erotic.

00:38:02 To do this, we must return to the site where the erotic papyrus may have been discovered.

00:38:08 It is an important settlement that was occupied by the workmen who built the Valley of the Kings.

00:38:16 Known as Deir el Medina it has provided key evidence for unlocking some of the mysteries of ancient sex.

00:38:22 >> PARKINSON: In Deir el Medina, we get a sense of the smut, we get a sense of the adultery, we get a sense of how people thought and felt about sex.

00:38:31 >> NARRATOR: Sources recovered from the village indicate that as many as 100 individuals lived in the community for much of its history.

00:38:39 >> MANNICHE: Here we are high above the village of Deir el Medina.

00:38:43 Over on the other side of the mountain is the Valley of the Kings.

00:38:47 And not only do we have the village here, but we also have the tombs of the workers who went to work in the Valley of the Kings to excavate and decorate the tombs.

00:38:59 >> NARRATOR: These construction workers and craftsmen left clues.

00:39:02 >> HUGHES: These workers were on a ten-day week, so they would go off and do their jobs, clearly building up a bit of sexual tension over those ten days and then come back and release themselves on their women.

00:39:13 Um, so, what you don't know is whether this is a kind of archaeological record of the actual sex lives of the workers or whether it's a kind of fantasy of... this is the perfect sex that you'd get after that long ten-day week.

00:39:25 >> NARRATOR: The ancient name of the site was Set Maat, “The Place of Truth.”>> ALAN LLOYD: It came into existence in the reign of Amenhotep I, perhaps sometime about 1520, 1510 BC and it existed for over 400 years.

00:39:42 >> NARRATOR: It is now viewed as a microcosm of Egyptian society.

00:39:46 >> MANNICHE: You would find people who were extraordinarily literate because they were scribes and artists, so compared to other villages all over Egypt, this is a very, very special place.

00:39:56 >> NARRATOR: The site has yielded a wealth of artifacts and texts that provide vital information about the way these people lived and how they viewed sex.

00:40:07 This papyrus has survived from the late New Kingdom period in around 1500 BC.

00:40:13 It reveals the sexual antics of an artisan.

00:40:16 It describes him sleeping with a married woman and her daughter, who is then passed on to his son.

00:40:23 >> LLOYD: And there is no site which provides as much information on daily life in ancient Egypt as this site does.

00:40:31 The site provides so much lasting archaeological information simply because the area surrounding the Valley of the Kings consists of limestone.

00:40:40 This provided the workmen with shards of rock that they could use as sketch books.

00:40:46 >> MANNICHE: In Deir el Medina have been found lots of flakes of limestone with wonderful drawings on them which the craftsman sat and did while they were having their time off when they were not working over on the Valley of the Kings.

00:41:00 >> NARRATOR: Known as ostrica, thousands have been found.

00:41:03 They have been proven to be fascinating and important slices of ancient history.

00:41:08 >> PARKINSON: This is a small flake of limestone from the village of Deir el Medina and on it, there's a doodle, a cartoon done by the workmen who decorated the tombs in the Valley of the Kings.

00:41:18 And it shows a man having sex with a woman and beside it, there is a line of hieroglyphs and she is saying, “Calm now is the desire of my skin.” And it seems to be a sort of parody of the religious scenes you see on temple walls.

00:41:34 >> NARRATOR: The craftsmen would use these pieces of rock as sketch books for their thoughts, thoughts which would reflect everyday life.

00:41:41 >> MANNICHE: Some of these drawings also have erotic scenes, people having sexual intercourse, uh, which is a very rare thing in Egyptian art, even in unofficial art.

00:41:50 But this is the place where these things would come from.

00:41:53 >> NARRATOR: Just like Egyptian statues, these images were subject to censorship through the ages.

00:41:59 Today, only a few remain on display to the public.

00:42:04 Hidden in a corner of an old cabinet in the Cairo Museum is a sexual representation that is both shocking and beautiful.

00:42:12 After persuading the museum, we were allowed to show this 3,000-year-old sketch on camera.

00:42:18 >> WAHEED EDWAR: Here we have some ostraca from Deir el Medina from Luxor.

00:42:23 And “ostraca,” it's a Greek word means, like, shell or, um, limestone flake.

00:42:29 And actually on this ostraca, the ancient Egyptian worker from Deir el Medina had sketched some of the daily life activities, like showing animals, showing kings, showing, you know, even relationship between man and women.

00:42:42 Like this one, for example, it shows a man and woman, uh, making love, and it's painted in black ink.

00:42:49 >> MANNICHE: The man is kneeling in front of the lady, and she is wrapping her legs, her thighs around his neck.

00:42:56 This must have been one of the favorite ones, because it has been depicted so often.

00:43:00 It's beautifully drawn, because not all of the pornographic drawings are very well drawn.

00:43:05 But this one, from an artistic point of view, it's also a very high quality.

00:43:10 >> NARRATOR: We begin to see a more common view of erotica in everyday life.

00:43:15 From another image recovered from Deir el Medina, we see a young woman wearing see-through clothes– a recurring image in Egyptian society.

00:43:24 >> LLOYD: Well, they represent women in linen garments.

00:43:28 They wear long linen garments in the New Kingdom.

00:43:31 They create the impression that you can see through the linen garments, which of course you couldn't.

00:43:37 But high-quality linen will cling to the shape of the body, and they therefore represent the ghost of the body underneath, which again indicates the interest in the female form.

00:43:53 >> NARRATOR: By studying ancient Egyptian love poetry, we can gain a further insight into the type of sexual fantasies that were prevalent in everyday society.

00:44:02 These texts reveal the sensual feelings of ancient Egyptians.

00:44:08 >> HUGHES: Around about 1,500 BC, we start to get evidence of this beautiful love poetry that ancient Egyptians would write to one another.

00:44:16 The men are all described as kind of superheroes, and the ideal woman emerges wet from the Nile with her clothes clinging to her body.

00:44:28 >> NARRATOR: Bettany Hughes discovers one reference to a fantasy that is just as evocative today.

00:44:34 >> HUGHES: This is one very good example of a bit of love poetry, which came from Deir el Medina.

00:44:40 It was written about 3,000 years ago.

00:44:41 It's a lover who's writing to his girlfriend, and he describes her perfect white breast, that she has fingers like lotus flowers.

00:44:50 He says, in her thighs her beauty rests.

00:44:53 And when she passes, all men turn their necks to look at her.

00:44:57 >> NARRATOR: All the clues come together to paint a vivid picture of the ultimate ancient Egyptian male fantasy: A beautiful and seductive young woman rising dripping wet from the sacred River Nile.

00:45:12 It's a seductive image we could easily see in a movie or advertisement today.

00:45:18 >> HUGHES: They were very sensitive.

00:45:20 And if the words are anything to go by, then some of them were clearly very skilled lovers, too.

00:45:27 >> NARRATOR: So if they had the same sexual appetite as we do, did the ancients also have the same voyeuristic desires?

00:45:36 Could the sexually explicit papyrus be the world's first men's magazine, the smoking gun that reveals the truth about sex in ancient Egypt?

00:49:04 > NARRATOR: The Turin Erotic Papyrus is one of the most sexually-explicit documents ever recovered from antiquity.

00:49:35 Yet its true meaning remains a mystery.

00:49:39 It's a code that needs to be cracked if we are to understand the truth about the real sex lives of the ancient Egyptians.

00:49:46 >> LLOYD: The Turin Erotic Papyrus is a document which some Egyptologists get very po-faced about.

00:49:54 They're clearly deeply embarrassed about this sort of thing.

00:49:58 But the plain fact is that the ancient Egyptian approach to sexuality was a great deal more relaxed than the attitudes that we find in current monotheistic societies.

00:50:10 >> NARRATOR: For much of its history, it's been kept under lock and key.

00:50:14 The previous curator at the Egyptian Museum in Turin placed a table in front of the artifact, so that no one could stare deep into its surface.

00:50:25 We have been afforded unique access to film the papyrus.

00:50:29 Historian Bettany Hughes has been fascinated by this artifact and is intrigued to see the object up close.

00:50:36 It is a shocking revelation for her.

00:50:39 >> HUGHES: What I'm looking at is completely unique in the world.

00:50:42 There's nothing else like this.

00:50:44 And it is a fantastic thing, because it's so beautiful, it's so beautifully produced.

00:50:48 But then when you get into it and see what the pictures are, this is where it becomes really intriguing, because this is basically Playboy magazine of the ancient world.

00:50:57 So there are 12 erotic scenes here, where elderly men are having a great time with young, beautiful Egyptian girls.

00:51:06 >> NARRATOR: The severely damaged papyrus has not been treated well by time.

00:51:10 Although sections are missing, there is enough fragmentary evidence to allow scholars to fill in this ancient jigsaw puzzle.

00:51:17 Using this information, we have restored the papyrus to its original state using computer graphics.

00:51:24 This is our depiction of the graphic images that the ancient Egyptians would have seen over three millennia ago.

00:51:30 >> PARKINSON: With something like the Turin Erotic Papyrus, it's very hard to know what it was used for.

00:51:36 It certainly wasn't written by peasant farmers.

00:51:39 It comes from very literate, sophisticated people.

00:51:44 Some modern scholars have thought it's a treatise on the art of lovemaking.

00:51:48 Some have suggested that it's a religious text.

00:51:51 >> NARRATOR: On one section of the papyrus are images of animals imitating human behavior, which has left some scholars to believe that the papyrus is meant to be humorous.

00:52:00 >> BOOTH: So whether this was someone's way of spending the hours in the evening– was to sketch this– or whether there was some deeper purpose, we don't really know.

00:52:09 >> NARRATOR: As the images come to life, various scenes are depicted showing sexual positions.

00:52:15 One sequence shows a woman having sex on a chariot– a mysterious image to scholars.

00:52:20 >> HUGHES: And I'm not completely sure what's going on here, 'cause this is a very rare image in ancient Egyptian art.

00:52:25 But I think what it probably is, is the chariot was a real symbol of prestige and power.

00:52:31 So probably what you've got is a conflation of sex and violence 3,200 years ago, just as we put the two together today.

00:52:40	>> NARRATOR: The woman's hair is being pulled by the old man.
00:52:43	Hair was very erotic in ancient Egypt.
00:52:46	>> BOOTH: Hair was one of the most erotic things a woman could have in ancient Egypt, especially in the New Kingdom, the 18th and the 19th Dynasty.
00:52:54	Most Egyptians shaved their heads so they were bald, as a way of getting rid of lice and other such horrible, noxious crawling things in your hair.
00:53:03	So they would wear these very elaborate wigs.
00:53:06	>> NARRATOR: Other Egyptian texts refer to hair.
00:53:08	One states, "Put your wig on and let's go to bed.">> BOOTH: The idea was that the bigger and more elaborate your wig, the sexier you were.
00:53:16	And in some of the 19th Dynasty love poetry, they do actually refer to women being so enamored with their loved one that they forget what they're doing, and they leave their hair half undone.
00:53:30	And it's the equivalent of being caught naked, really, to have– be caught with your wig only half-prepared.
00:53:36	>> NARRATOR: Our ideas of rock and roll hedonism also seem to be present in the papyrus-.
00:53:41	young girls servicing aging men while high on drugs.
00:53:45	>> EXELL: We see images of scantily-clad young ladies involved in the sexual act.
00:53:50	On the top of their heads depicted is a lotus flower.
00:53:55	Now, clearly they aren't wearing these lotus flowers, but the lotus flowers are symbols.
00:53:59	And what we learn from seeing these lotus flowers is that these young women are under the influence of the narcotic that could be extracted from the lotus flower.
00:54:08	And so what we are to understand by that is that these women are open to enjoying the sexual act.
00:54:15	>> NARRATOR: With evidence of drugs, alcohol, music and aging men, are we looking at an ancient brothel?
00:54:22	>> HUGHES: I suspect this is a brothel.
00:54:24	I mean, there's a lot of sexual action going on here.

00:54:26 And it'd be hard to imagine this was just a normal night out in Bronze Age Egypt.

00:54:32 Interestingly, actually, if this is a brothel, then the prostitutes of course wouldn't have been paid in money, 'cause there wasn't cash at this time.

00:54:37 So they'd have been paid for their services in something like fish or maybe a bushel of wheat.

00:54:43 >> NARRATOR: But what evidence is there of prostitutes in ancient Egypt?

00:54:47 >> BOOTH: It's very likely prostitutes existed.

00:54:50 As they say, it's the oldest profession in the world.

00:54:53 We do have snippets of information that could suggest prostitution existed– one being the Turin Erotic Papyrus, which could be a story of a New Kingdom brothel in Thebes.

00:55:06 >> NARRATOR: Can we answer the burning questions?

00:55:08 Who was the papyrus made for?

00:55:11 What was it for?

00:55:12 >> MANNICHE: There's a huge debate about what is the significance of the Turin Erotic Papyrus.

00:55:18 We have 12 different positions of intercourse.

00:55:21 Some would like to relate it to the world of the gods.

00:55:24 Others say that it's a Thebeen priest having a night out in a brothel or something like that.

00:55:30 But very likely, it's either a piece of early pornography– the clue here is actually the text that's written in between the figures, because that gives scraps of the conversation that the parties are having.

00:55:44 >> NARRATOR: One image shows a woman pleasuring herself on an ancient pot known as an amphora.

00:55:49 She paints her lips as she does so.

00:55:51 The text next to this picture is still visible.

00:55:54 >> HUGHES: At first glance, what you see is that she's applying lipstick.

00:55:58 She's kind of dabbing it on with a long brush, staring into a mirror.

00:56:02 And that in itself was an erotic act in Egypt, because mirrors often had handles in the shape of a beautiful woman.

00:56:08 But then, when your eye moves down, you see that it gets really quite pornographically raunchy.

00:56:14 That actually, this young girl is sitting with her legs wide apart on top of an amphora, which is turned upside down so the point is inserted inside her.

00:56:23 So she's obviously pleasuring herself on this vase.

00:56:25 And from the expression on her face, it's working.

00:56:29 It's actually very interesting, because what's written here is that she's saying to this old man who's with her in this scene, "You give me nothing, so I've got to resort to this," to the vase to give her her orgasm.

00:56:40 And then just down here, you can see, it's very fragmentary, it's very broken.

00:56:43 You can just about read out.

00:56:44 She's kind of saying, "Come here, big boy, dirty boy, you kind of sex criminal." And he's obviously enjoying this moment, because he's got a huge engorged phallus which is resting just next to the amphora.

00:56:57 >> NARRATOR: Ultimately, the evidence suggests the Turin Erotic Papyrus may be the world's oldest men's pornographic magazine.

00:57:03 >> LLOYD: The artist is representing sexual activity with enormous enthusiasm and with lots of salacious detail.

00:57:11 I think that he would be a bit like those characters you used to find in Cairo in the old days, who'd sidle up to you and say, "Hey, mister, you want to see a dirty picture?" I very much like the idea that this is a kind of precursor of Playboy.

00:57:28 >> NARRATOR: We may never determine who precisely created the Turin Erotic Papyrus and for what purpose.

00:57:35 What we do know is that 3,000 years later, experts regard it as one of the most important artifacts of antiquity.

00:57:42 >> HUGHES: The priceless thing about this papyrus is that it allows you to decode real Egyptian sexuality.
00:57:49 I mean, this is a way that you can understand how the Ancient Egyptians had sex, what they enjoyed doing, and what was just a little bit dangerous and naughty for them.
00:57:59 >> NARRATOR: At the end of our journey, mysteries still remain about sex in ancient Egypt.
00:58:04 But by decoding their imagery, we have pieced together a more complete picture.
00:58:08 The Turin Erotic Papyrus is a lens.
00:58:11 It provides a stunning new view into the civilization that created it, shedding light on their beliefs on the afterlife, rituals of fertility and attitudes toward erotica.
00:58:20 An intimate view of sex in the ancient world.

KUNDALINI EXAMPLE

Stella 55001 is giving a hieroglyphic example of the Egyptian concept of how the kundalini is opened. The reason that the Egyptologist could not read it is because it is written in the secret sacred Egyptian priesthood language. I have told you now what it is. I do not think that it would be right to tell you exactly what the sequence says at this time. On the other hand, maybe I should. You do know that this is the knowledge of the pharaohs called The Nagas?

BEGINNING CIPHER

The First thing that we have to remember is that in many cases artwork is encoded with special messages for a certain group of people. In some cases, one piece of artwork can have several different meanings depending on who is looking at it and that person's given level in what might be called a "mystery" system. The system that I am going to discuss here is that of ancient Egypt.

The reason for this discussion is to decipher the piece of artwork called the Turin 55001 papyrus stela.

The first thing we have to do is dissect the Egyptian religious system. We need to look at the concept of life after death. The Egyptian philosophy was one that believed in a ritual that was designed to help the deceased person "cross over" into the after life. The ritual was called "the opening of the mouth' ceremony. We must be clear that this procedure was for a dead person. In the artwork about the ritual, you generally see a mummy and strange gods that help the dead to the promised land called the after life.

The way the system worked was that the deceased person's spirit was made ready for the trip into the after life by first mummifying the body. This was a very elaborate process. After a certain amount of time, the mummified body was placed in a tomb. In many cases, the process of the trip was painted on the tomb walls. The priest had spell books that they often put in the tomb with the deceased. In the Egyptian philosophy, there is considered to be an amount of time before the spirit "breaks away" from the body. All of this process has been documented extensively.

Many people are aware that the Egyptians were concerned with the motions of the stars. We are talking about astronomy. It is important to note that The Great Pyramid of Giza is said to contain alignments to certain stars. One might go as far as to refer to The Great Pyramid as a star gate. I could go further into this concept, but this is not the subject of this writing.

The Egyptians had an advanced knowledge of "a" zodiac system. I make note of "a" zodiac system because the symbolism that the Egyptians used is not the same as today's generally accepted hieroglyphic system. Recently the current zodiac system has had a shake up. There was a said "finding" of a thirteenth zodiac sign. That sign is called Ophiuchus. Its hieroglyphic is a man holding a serpent or snake. The strange thing about this is that this symbolic star hieroglyphic has been known for a long time. In our current system, we just did not use it as a major sign.

ADAMIC GENESIS

I thought I had written my greatest work a few days ago. It involved the theory of a visible electromagnetic signature forming above The Great Pyramid. The theory put a lot of pieces into place about many strange facts and concepts I had read over the last ten or so years. I was so happy to have been finished "my work", or so I thought! March 16, 2005, I was looking up some information about a biblical subject I had given instruction upon. Then I began to panic. Oh no, I think I misstated a Bible fact. Not that I can't, but it bothered me. I was in the process of writing "MIRACLE OF ADAM", which became "IMAGE OF NACHASH"! So with the name change, I needed to know how to spell Nachash. So I grabbed the "Dictionary Of Jewish Lore and Legend" by Alan Unterman. Then I looked for the word time and time again. I knew it was in the book. I had seen it. The more I looked, the more I could not find it. What in the world is going on? I can't believe this! Has my mind skipped time or what? So in disbelief, I began to flip the pages of the book. Now I began to challenge my own core theory about the origin of Adam. To be more accurate Adam Kadmon. My theory, my theory, it was all falling apart. Where had I gotten my crazy theory from anyway? I felt stupid. It was as if I had awakened from a bad dream called life. Which way is up. So in a frenzy, I kept looking for that word in the "n" section. Then I just started to flip the pages and look at the images. I came across this strange of Adam as a statue. I thought: "What is this all about?" Look how big the head is. Look at the strange size of the body features. It is just strange; the figure of Adam being a hermaphrodite is in question. Where had I got this "stuff" from? I began to question myself as some "people" I used to know "had"! And then I saw it. Oh no. No! This can't be. Flash, inside my mind! Do I dare, and if so by what authority? Can I do such a thing? I had recently concluded that Eve was taken from one of the four paths about the central core of a five path kundalini system. But what about my concept of Adam as having been created euthric? How does dust turn into flesh? And is that flesh the same as the clothing of animal skins. Wham, I can feel it! Oh the power, the surge; I began to move. And then I thought of a particular scene in the "Power Rangers" movie where the crushing blow of final victory was issued. And the final words of "The Beaten One", whom represents the enemies and false accusers said:"Oh No!" And in great joy, I began to dance. Dance like David. Oh, I need to be very clear about my last comment. When I say "David", I mean King David of The Bible whom danced, and was criticized for it by his wife, after he came back from "beating The Lords enemies"! Royal David of The Bible! And so I danced, for I had never had a thought like this. Finally, I thought of my teacher, Great Uncle Sim; boy would he be laughing while saying:"For what you want, you are going to have to suffer!" At this point, if he was still here, I would agree that he was right; but, then I would add:"I believe the word you are trying to pronounce is "sefirah"<see fire ra ah ha>! Then would could both enjoy the joke. I think he was correct in telling me to strengthen myself with the knowledge of The Word; while implying that if I make myself ready, when "they" come a leaning upon me, "they" will know not as to whom "they" are talking to. Beware of the strange mess of familiar doctrines. So of what they have to say is as "the yeast" of the world! Yelp! On to it, it's been a long time coming, but it's hot now.

TO MYSELF

Sometimes you start alone. Sometimes you cried alone. You kept the vision. You kept hold to the plan. You used both to hold on to your faith. Oh how many days did I hear you crying, but saying how could you expect for anyone else to do what you have not done yourself! You didn't betray yourself along the path. And you tried harder than anything I ever thought you had up inside of you. I have never seen such a fumbling bumbling bucket carrying flat footed long winded last place underdog type come across the finish line so hard. Don't forget to remember the laughter you caused in them who watched you struggle along the way. Don't forget their kind words of reassurance "Of You Foolishness" along the way! Listen here boy, yes you, Frank, Meta, or whatever; you make sure you break out in laughter also. Laugh, laugh, laugh, and laugh some more! If I had wings, I would wrap them around you, me, and us; which is I! Amazing!

THE STAGE

In the world, there is a great stage called "Step On Up"! It is an open invitation to come and be tested at anytime you wish. Many have come before me. You can choose your subject of so- called expertise; but beware the critics and crowd goes hard upon them with theories. On the sage, all of it is upon the line. Many have left broken and beaten. And so, I, Meta step upon that stage to first answer the basic standard questions, then put forth my theories and defend it to the masters of the world. My friend Frank gives me, Meta, a last pep talk. He recites some of my favorite lines on enthusiasm that he knows help get us here. "This is the moment that we have all been waiting for". "Down, down, down from the mountains yee come, onto the battle front ye go, you shall fight in the hill sides, you shall fight upon the plains, you shall fight upon the sea shores; and Never Surrender", "This is all your love, this is all your pain", "it is not a machine, it is as a man, therefore you have to punch some more; then you have to punch some more, now go knock the bum out cause Mikey loves ya", and your gonna dance, you're gonna dance, you're gonna dance, float like the butterfly, but sting like the bee, rumble young man rumble"! The chants bring tears to my eyes for in silence I now know the day and moment is upon me again. One last look back at "Yesterday". I can even hear the song. My lower eye lids well up as if my tears were about to flood the world. As I wipe my eyes and cover my face with a tissue, I notice a great heat starting to increase in my chest. A heat that is changing the rhythm of my breath. My nostrils are starting to dry from the heat of my exhale. My upper nasal cavity is starting to open when I inhale to allow large amounts of cool air to enter my chest. I have known this pattern before. Oh yes, I am getting ready to perform. My forehead is starting to wrinkle, as I step both feet upon the stage, I began to close my focus like unto the eyes of The Great Lion about to strike upon a greasy pig. The pig will scream out due to the strike of my paw ripping his flesh open and tearing his bones apart. Then the sound will be my signature, known by my former enemies of which has not been heard in the jungle for years. I shall call forth the sound of my roar before I bite. And so the jungle becomes aware again. Just then Frank starts yelling to and at me: "Open your wings, open your wings, and cut the limit control on. The Mental Meta Drive to "Off"! Off means full and maximum power which is called "Maximus"! His last words: "Consume and be beautiful-I love you, you have been my champion. Now do it one more time, as a tear falls from my left eye for knowing what he is about to say, for "The Gipper"!

PRESENT YOURSELF

And so, I stand upon the stage to present myself. First I have to answer some basic and standard questions. Everyone has to do it no matter what topic they choose. My stage or pen name of choice is Meta 3.14. I have come to represent myself. I have come alone, Mono est Mono. I am self taught. My weapon of choice is called "The Twelves"! I have come due to my own personal inspiration based upon something in specific that I have read. And that is basically it. They then connect the holographic image projection helmet to my head so that my mental images can be seen upon the large screens by all in attendance. As the final attachment is made, I look over to my left and images start to jump in and out upon the screen. I see some of my friends that I made during my journey in my mind's eye! Suddenly, there I am standing upon an empty dance floor waiting for the "final jam" to start. Look, I've got on my mystical dancing shoes. Bernita yells out "awh shucks now", Aunt T says "Tiger", Momma Helen says "The Brown Bomber", Daddy "C" says "You can hit the ball, Joe". Wait a minute; they are looking into my mind; if they want to do that they should read my writing. "Shields on and reverse the poles". "Enough of the preamble even thought I had much more to say!"

THE THEORY

I step to the podium upon the stage of life and announce my intended subject. Respectfully, members of the world stage community, I would like to present: "An interpretation of Adam and the Garden" by Frank M. Conaway, Jr. And the crowd goes wild, the crowd goes wild! Half of them are bewildered with disbelief. My friends from Howard University School of Architecture go off. "Here he goes, here he goes!" I look over at them, then strike the pose from "The Acrylic Beam Project"! Thompson, well, to hear his version of it to come is to say "special" at the least! Karate Master Eddie Butcher starts laughing and saying: "Here comes The Grape Stomper, one of the ruckus brothers!" Look on the screen, it is grandmaster Butcher: "Now, now, now, it went down just as I planned it!" Sr. Master Butcher comments: "Crazy Horse!" Hay, it is Mark "Big Daddy" Goldmedalist, and we laugh at the Rocky show. Forward on, to "the throw down"! Fully ready, I am ready! Wow I know the day would come if I just held on. Letting go was no option, not for me. A final question from the panel: "So where are all your sources and resources to attempt such a thing?" Did I hear the word "Attempt"! So again I throw up the sign of "The Acrylic Beam Project"! The Howard home team goes wild! They know what it is going to be. Rob would call it "A Classic"! Rick Lu is about to start telling them! Guy Morton says: "It's about us!" Old Feet Of Flame just has that look on his face. See, the Z28 with the Meta Pops Racer super street sleeper, custom designed by Meta "full" roller cam. Getting ready to go "wide and open"! In that "Flat Foot The Grape Stomper' Con ugly, ultimate Champion of White Belt division at Willie Bens Baltimore "Karate" Wars winner? Yes, the crowd goes wild! "A Day In Thee Life, Part Two!" Show them what you got. And so I respond by telling the judges and audience that I shall prove my theory by using "one book"! The judges begin to discuss the ridiculous nature of me even being there. Did I hear the word "fool" and "Bum"! Johnny O said: "Oh yah!" Look, there is Mr. Haus and there Mrs. Aronoff. Wow, all my teachers flash upon the screen, even Professor "if you haven't read it" Doctor Jones. "Model that thing" he says. And then my main man, I like your locks and good looking out baby, word up and rolling. P.S. Thank you for allowing me to run the prelude in your class. Oh ya, it is on the legend level. But that was the days before "they" set it off. They ain't seen a set off yet- Cosmic Meta! I can write this because of what I am about to do! I can name that tune and support it in "One Book"! Dancing breaks out, calling Doctor Bone, calling Doctor Bone! You must understand, that if I go to the next level I can be allowed all sorts of special whatevers! Ya, I like that-Ike Love Baby, Ike Love! Let's get it on, my first and most major slow dance, well that and My Ebony Princess! They call him Acapulco Frank. I hear my friends: Pup Pup, Little Dummy, Bradford Street, Raji, Snow, Ice, Crush, and Mrs. Missy barking. They are my dogs let loose. Then there is very special Maw Maw, the only cat I ever loved. Oh Lord, and the turtle died! To Sojourner, Douglass, Howard University, Morgan State University, Northwestern "Wildcats" High, Fallstaff Middle, Lexington Terrace Elementary, Hernwood Elementary, and Homewood Elementary. To all my teachers in all of the arts and ways. To all whom have helped me and but did not betray. To all of them that I found clues in their books. To them whose music I needed. To Supreme <super me> Master of The Twelves <more than one 1200 turntable>, Wayne of O'Dells! To suffer on the Twelves, a sound to hear, followed by Maniac "I Bex" McCloud! Truly turn table terror! To the "Street Racers" and V.W. Martin. To all of them whom loved me and didn't put theirs above me! We came to the floor to get down. Look, my first car dad gave me. Thanks "M". To my sisters, and all of them whom I called "Moms"! Every tear of it! I'm coming in hot and hard. It's a Baltimore thing. Pull out your maps and map this. The sign of "The Acrylic Beam Project", an architectural wonder in itself! The Big Payback! A special hello to Bootzy and The Mother Ship Mob. Let me not forget my metaphysical teachers and then I called out, Hay Bobby, you never sent me those papers, but I understand man. Nubia and Booty: "Wow"! Like as if I were your own son! To Tai Chi and The Master of Tai Chi, thank you for letting me ride. To the Northwestern J. V. Lacrosse team, I raise the sign of The Stick. To Windbush for teaching me to ride while chopping. To The Champions Karate School and the Kussoth Dojo! To Aunt Cozette and Uncle Tom, Bless you both! Smile down upon me. To my friends, and even adversaries. As I have heard it said: "How do you like me now?" And to the hidden master of The One Thousand Stroke of the Chimbar technique, I like it, I really do! Bruce Lee is also remembered: "Will this be the same song that we will be singing tomorrow?" Well, will it? Not if, as in White belt division I am the last man standing, again! Bring the NOISE Meta, bring it! "And he entered onto the field", that's what they said! To Damo, the "Black Indian Sage Monk" of who it is said that you taught the Shaolin monks the way back after going into the depths called Zen. To my martial students whom showed me love and respect. To "Mantis Knights", and I knew when I heard the Kia! Hay to Tarry Cooper, ah, my producer? To the maple tree. To LL, Kel El, and Frank; listen to the sounds of my wings ya'll! Cool J, Rino, and Funk O Man! To you, what can I say, "your sailor"? Sunny, of the Ladret crew, I can feel it in the air tonight! What kind of goings on are these? To the producer of my first rap song that went triple gold platinum. Oh that track was called "One These"! To Shystiville and them, bang on! To the S E S crew, and big head "captured by the aliens Ed"! Wave yo hands side to side, now do the roll back! To all of yall, and RACECAR50. Now, I shall begin to teach! Most and highest of all to he and him that answered my call and cry from the darkness, and said that unto little old me: "How is it that one can see and hear so far?" Oops, my bad! And Metatron! Meta 3.14

OPENING THE CORE

And so, we now have several different versions of what is said to have happened at a place called "The Garden of Eden". And so, it appears to be very clear, except that the "inner" teaching still don't agree with the base story. Questions upon questions still arise! Translation upon interpretation come forward, but to them whom have studied the three major cultures in question and can answer the question of revelations 13:18, it is not complete! And so, first I would like to start with what is said from The Bible called Genesis about the creation and what happened that is called "The Fall". That is as far as I am going with this, other than to explain a possible answer to that which might be called "The Error of

Unwise Adam" from the vantage point of criticism after an act has been done. Yes, I can truly say that in my own life I may have, on a scale, experienced a similar drama. But due to my forewarning I was able, in greatest pain known to me, to rise above the stumbling stone called "worst than Death itself"! Hail Glory! If it were not apart of my testing and instruction, what by the name of God himself could it have been? Oh, on this point and that, I could tell you! But no need, for as it is written, and so, I saw it, by testing it for myself, for what it is and was and still appears to be! And so, it is written that man shall not live by bread along. Now I would like to dissect this that has been handed down for years via one of the major cultures inner sayings found in **Ask Me**.

DEAR f(x) FRIEND

Even if it is not put to print, because I have produced it through and by: "the yod" called hand, it is still valid! Dear- Friend, I hope you have had a nice trip. And so, when was it that the thousand years was due to be up: one thousand A.D. or what? According to my calculations, it should be about one thousand A.D. that was and holding time, plus the sentence of one thousand years. That makes the time about the year two thousand. But wait; remember the six B.C. issue; so that makes it about 1994. Now if we add your core denominator to that, it becomes about the year 2000 A.D. Who knows? And what about the sign of Hale and Boop, the comet, hum? But traveling at the speed of sound, a cosmic "gong", when pieces of the Kermit comet, as in Egypt, hit the planet Saturn; did that cause a sonic vibration to release unleash you again upon the world. Oh Great Winged Wicked One, be happy, for your servants have been busy, as in a chess game. But lo, they have left your name and sign upon their works. It is your people! Yes you trained them into this way, rejoice! What a great "people" you have under the control of your mind set. Now, as far as the pray is concerned, you won't believe this, so I'll let you review the tapes from that called "The House of David"! Being, when you see this, stand as I do and have done. Oh no, oh yes! Did you not know that if, and you were, you were defeated before; the lame, cripple, and broken had a chance. Oh perverted teacher, thy pray half become thy's predator! You have draw upon yourself the angry male lion called "The Clown" or "It"! Two thousand years of training fueled by your excellent teachings. But not upon the limited battle field called life, but unto the next level of which ye know, but we and them have come to Believe. Did you not take the remaining seven thousand! Wonder what they were up to? Laying in wait, for you "Oh Great One"! Yes, seeing, eyes opened since the first perverted day. Looking for the source of "beauty" that causes it! Why it's been called by your many names now purified into your once great name! Ah, did you enjoy your stay? Anyway, it appears that an old old friend of yours is waiting to see you! You know him! The one with no name, so "they" say! Ha, Ha, Metatron! Say what? Well no, they and them have been training for the day of your judgement. At first they knew not why, old tempter. Then they heard of "your friend Job"! Wow, you were classic buddy! Then they found out about your "Entity" fondness of females. Really? Then they found out about the tricks and treat you play and had laid upon children. Oh it gets better. The young adults began to find out how you "get down"! Real funky they say about you. Hold on, they even made records and tapes about your "virility". Your potency is known throughout the world for ages. Why even your children are famous! Yes, they are called Giants or <nephilim>. I know you like that. But I need to tell you. I know of a certain person, him and them, of who have been watching you for a long time; even unto "The Garden"! I think they used some sort of metaphysical induction unit called "a trap" to cause you to act in "unseen ways"! I think the shepherd was disguised as a wolf, and the wolf as a sheep. But the sheep was no wolf, but one that has been trained by the shepherd. They and them laid in wait for you! And you can, causing that which you do, and might I say do well. But the sheep did not take unto your heavy hand well. Lo, and so, they cried out unto the sky, and so, in a short time down looked towards The Moon! And you know what, it, That Sheep told on you! Yes it did. And suddenly he, him, I heard, it was Metatron that was dispatched to teach him, and so I heard what they have planned for unto you! I heard them in union and I was feared to move Oh Great Winged Wicked One! Now seeing that yee are at the final move, they planned to catch you, again, in ASSUNDER!

Then your great powers will be striped from you since you have been cut off from your tree. And that of the other tree has been given by your first captor. Then he, that sheep, began to "confess against you" to him also as hidden. And what that one said unto "The Hidden" is unspeakable. Yet I heard the confession "Of Sights", but I could not remember it, for it was covered with an advance device. It was terrible, all that was said! But "your" name came up often and frequent. As if he was some sort of hunter, not, a luster of one specific type: "You"! And it seems that it, the sheep, watched its flock. And when the poachers came in your name; it went down, even unto Egypt and stood in front of a great sword tip, knelt down, and I saw him write: "I have come as the act of 'Repent'". That is what it wrote in front of that image. Then it Ran! Lo, I ran first when I saw what it was doing. Strange things and acts from books. Clearly, it had focused upon your name and hide. And I heard just a few things that it said before I ran. It said: "Oh, if I am granted the power to grasp it about the throat, and then flatten my foot to kick it in the groins. Oh, if I can grasp the sword that turns every which a way, and control it by mind intention! Oh mighty Cherubim, if thy thirst. I will let from it that which is stolen! Call down, call down; they and them, turn to see, the least whip and kick a larger greater. Break open the seal of the gate. Move aside that who chained before, for this time no chain is needed. Great fierce sayings and names of ancient issue before. With the hand, feet, and elements does come the links. Rolling greatly does the crowd cheer! Look, a splinter from the mail, "Victory"! Then its ethric size greatly increases, and you were amazed. But its attitude then greatly increased its progression. Suddenly it returned in form, but the function was as if all it had consumed. In closing it said: "If thy poachers come unto the Zoo, and yet ye I escape; and so, the hunter has become the hunted! When I sink my ethric tooth in I shall draw out and spit it upon the Earth. It is personal and game! "It had a Bad to the Bone attitude as if it sought you for the sport of it. It came to a point it called "Ready"! And it was, there! Excuse me, my great friend, but I have to go, and it wanted you to know Why! Remember That! P.S. And don't think when it remembered you, being about "The Great Well", it won't come visit you! Oh no it said! At its pleasure ascend and descend; whipping and kicking. INRA. Oh, in running,

I did hear, and so, when it hears certain tunes, sounds, or others; or even worst, if it sips, ye and yell, ye all; it goes unto something called "The Remembrance" and turns unto "you" and comes with its sayings and falling outs to visit! It plans to visit you, regularly, so that you remember and feel that which is ASSUNDER, even if afterward seems is not, perversion. Terrible is "its way", it thirst, unquenchable! The name in cipher upon its forehead, written by it in the day called its life! You and "you"! Of who is this that is recorded, and his master in feeling cut him a loose! It wants you, repent or not! That is its degree! Calculate that, its one and only request! Hail Mary, come quick see, etc. etc. How long will this goings on be going on? Time appears not to be an "issue" upon the realm of them that have by just reason and cause "risen up"! Could it be that it is upset about one single dust mite, how simple is it? Be it so, it is simple. A simple word: "Mines"! And hence!!!! Then, now, then, unto! The least and last element of Man and it, beyond that which is called time. The ultimate task master: "Toil the soil all the days of thy life", and if it lives forever-ye are toiled and over turned as he and called man perceives. Over, over and over again, but deeper each time until that which yee cannot produce is produced. Infinite upon the soil called your hide. What a wonder grace land. A place that can't ever be ripped up, but can rest from it. "Your Hide and Buttocks"! Oh, here is your, your, one like you through perversion, your mate! Him, and it is mated to the talking donkey day long, tilling your hide. Count your strides, and it shall count its rows! But it will be back! Play with it, tricks are for kids. Shame upon it, no, release the gardener upon the rebellious soil. All he sees is soil. If the Earth cries, so what? And what! Break "The Word" if ye can! Temptation, no, I dare you! Come on, step up – all call; phony, fronting, slacker, faker, bogus, backstabber, double dealing, two faced zodiac, sham artist, etc. Call it down, "good", but you miss, then it may grab it and deliver it unto you as the Elohim has said to be saying. Knock, knock, it's for you-symbolic Egyptian doorpost! See you, time, time and times again! When I read the record, my mouth becomes dry, is there no water in the Earth. Let me go and dig a well! On these!

MAXIMUS

And so upon thee day of the return of the glimpse of "Maximus", and yet so; although unto this day I did not realize, when Maximus twas, and yet unto so; they and them; laughed. Although, I tried to help them, they laughed and said "he was funny"! Do you know him and also another as that. But yee can click. And as to the Dog; sissy young dog; yee have let thee Maximus a loose! Oh sissy! Oh you are very what ever now! But "someone" has seen you! You and your root! Your friend, Maximus; mono est! "One more move, like it, beware of the Ace in the hold! "Brother not!" Be aware of what your and "another" master told you about it! Only once! False Lamb! P.S. You, as I heard, ain't never seen him Trip!

THEY ATE

And so, it is said that Eve and Adam did eat The Fruit that was of the forbidden. Now if we use the diagram of the sefirotic structure for Adam, and the straight seven fold path of Shushma for the structure of Eve; we should be able "to see" a variance from the sefirotic super structure of Adam Kadmon. And we do. Let's start with Eve. If we use the straight seven chakras or sefirots as Eve's energy core, in the science of kundalini we see the path is wavy. Why is the path wavy and not straight? Because of discord! The central path has been caused to waver. Normally we think this frequency action is a natural occurrence. But, the standing columnar wave technology explains this discord is not natural; but part of the resultant of variance, or disturbance. And that is what happened. Eve's inner core was set into a non harmonic vibration. Now as to Adam. I realized in the science of kundalini that the images and diagrams that are called standard are not of one, but of two "different" systems! Yes and No. One system is that of Eve, while the other system is of Adam; but both being subsets of The Adam Kadmon serfirotic super structure of "Adam him her them"! Proof? From "The Power of Kabbalah" by Yehuda Berg. These are words and written concepts, but it is said that a picture is worth one thousand words. Oh if we could find a picture. But and so I did, I knew it when I saw it, and then also describing it! Look, look at the cover of “The Chakras” by C.W. Leadbearter. Notice how the wheels or chakras are not in a vertical line after the point of the throat? Notice that the displacement point, if we over lay the cover with the sefirotic super structure of Adam Kadmon, is moved towards the weakest point. That of the removal of “Eve’s sefirot”. Now go to figure one on page 6, then “The Chakras according to Gichtel on page 17 plate 7, The Streams of Vitality on page 17 plate 8, and The Chakras And The Nervous System on page 40 plate one compared to the open path on page 33. Notice how page 40 plate one shows a crossing “x”, or tangle at the “solar plexus area located in the lumbar spinal ganglion! Is this not the area of the “removed” sefirotic sub-structure Eve tree of the Adam Kadmon sefirotic super structure? Yes it is! And here is your problem. In simple, Adam is said to leave his mother and father to cling into that woman Eve. Eve is not said to leave her family’s ways or traditions to rebound to Adam. So you have a formula that has two independent variables competing for the same position. But to give the answer, we must turn to another force. We see this “force” in action upon page 181 of “Dictionary of Jewish Lore and Legend by Alan Unterman. It is called “shekhinah”. At this point it should be said that Adam Kadmon was created in the image of his creator. Now is his creator has the correct sefirotic super structure still intact, two things are implied.<Hebrews 3:7-6:12> <Hebrews 12:12-13> Immutable Seed Theory Source <1 Corinthians, 1-2:16, 4:1-2, 9:21-27, 12, 14, 15, 2 Corinthians 4,5,11,>

PRAYING

A certain person asked me my opinion about something they had been asked. A person was preaching and lying on hands, but the person whom was preaching could not walk long due to being overweight. So someone whom noticed this asked why if they could heal others, they could not heal themselves? The comment was made about others praying for them the preacher. I thought about it. Then using Biblical principals I figured that the self prayer might not be specific enough. In other words, a person might pray that they could lose some weight. Now if the reason is not to "draw out" a certain person, then the motive behind the pray might be out of focus. I figure the prayer should be something like: "Oh Lord, now that all have seen me weak and broken down, return me unto a better state so that I may proclaim and profess The Power and The Glory of You!" Then they should start their work along the path to show what The Lord has done!

EXPLAIN WHY

Then I began to explain why one should read their Bible first before receiving study class. And the objection was leading to The 102nd reason I had ever heard for not reading the whole Bible. I used the example of grade school versus college teaching. In grade school the teacher gives examples and works thru new concepts. But in college this relationship is usually reversed. The instructor usually gives reading assignments, then requires work done upon the material read. After the student has done this, the instructor will generally instruct upon the subject. This is the development of "the independent" thinker. Just imagine a Physics professor trying to teach a middle school science student astrophysics concepts. Does it make any sense; I asked "No it does not!"

102 REASON

Then came the big one. A new reason as to why not to read The Bible: "Won't The Lord accept a person whether they read The Bible or not?" Great point. "Yes The Lord will accept you whether you read it or not!" "But the problem is not "The Lord", the problem is the body entity called Satan and The Devil!" You see, Satan and The Devil will use any trick possible to cause you to stumble. In one of the specialized priest groups, that is how they capture The Devil and Satan! Now we know the example of The Garden. But suppose Adam was aware of the scriptures during The Garden drama. It may have happened like this.

TEACH BROTHER

Ah ha, a chance to teach. Well now, here it is and here it comes. Example One: Eve comes to Adam with The Snake. Eve has not eaten of The Fruit. Adams response in weakness: yelling loudly "LORD"! That is Adam on medium "Milk". Adam on weak milk running while yelling "LORD"! Adam on strong "milk": he looks at Eve and yells "Run"! Then while running yells "LORD"! Adam on high power "milk": he grabs hold of Eves arm, pulls her while yelling "Run"! As they run, if she runs, Adam yells: "LORD"! Example Two. Eve and The Snake come to Adam, but Eve has not eaten of "The Fruit"! Adam on "meat": "Eve did you tell The Snake what The Lord told us? You did, and what exactly was that?" Eve tells Adam. "Un hun, and Snake is that what Eve told you? And The Snake responses "Yes"! "And Snake is that what you responded with? And The Snake says "Yes"! Oh, I see, yelling "LORD"! Adam on weak "meat": Adam looks at The Snake, then looks at Eve and begins to give her a lecture about not listening to Snakes, and listen to what The Lord had told them. This lecture goes on until The Lord comes back to The Garden. Adam walks up to The Lord to hear to hear if he has anything else to instruct upon. Then Adam says loudly: "Oh Lord, might I ask yee a question? The Lord says:"Sure Son"! Adam says, while looking at Eve:"Oh Lord, have you not told Eve and me about "The Forbidden Fruit"? The Lord says: "I have thus told you Adam and you Eve!" Adam pauses then says: "Oh Lord, would you mind telling Eve and I again lest one of us forget! "Wow! But my favorite: Example Three Adam on "Priest Meat". There is two parts to this example. The first part is if has not eaten of "The Fruit", and the second part is Eve has eaten of "The Fruit"! This is the basic "Priest Meat" response to the drama whether Eve has eaten or not. And so, here comes Eve and The Snake up to Adam to explain how wonderful "The Fruit" is! And so Eve and The Snake explain their point. Adams response: "And so, my name is Adam. I Adam was originated created "he, her, them"! I am Adam of whom I was gifted to name each and every animal based upon what was placed inside me. I named you "Snake"! <End of part one and two together> Part one continued. Now as to you, Eve, why don't you go and freshen up while I have a chat with this fellow The Snake! And so Eve left. Then Adam said unto The Snake: "Did you ever read about how they invented Baseball? "And The Snake said: "No!" Adam said: "Well, I just happen to have a souvenir in my back pocket, and look, your standing between Home Plate and First Base!" Part two continued. "But Eve has eaten The Fruit"! And so, Adam began to cry and sob. There he was, Adam, crying and weeping saying nothing. Then Adam finished crying. And so Adam began to speek. "I now, somehow know that you are not snake, but a Serpent! You see, I happened to have been over by that old rock sometime ago when it moved. Suddenly, there was a book. And so, I took a little break to look into the book. The more I read, the more interesting it became. I learned about so many things. But I found some parts of the book awakening. So I decided to jump into the Cherubim chariot and go forward into a place called Egypt. Then I went way forward to about a time called Tuesday March 29, 2005 A.D. I happened to meet some guy they call Meta! I asked him about a certain person named Adam. I explained to him how I was Adam, but then he explained to me how The Lord is the first Adam. It was all so confusing. Then I read his book. It was even worse. I found out the The Lord is the groom, then who is the bride. He explained how I was, but I figured that somehow my sefirotic super structure must fit into The Lords Grand Sefirotic Super Structure. I found the concept very interesting. I also found this Meta guy very interesting. I wanted to understand him, so I asked him some questions. I explained how I had been down in Egypt learning about Baseball. I'll get back to that issue late. Now in the book I found every so often, a name was missing. So often, a name was missing. So I really wondered about who the book was speaking? So I explained to Meta who I was, and he began to share something with me. I found out that he had been a teacher of a very special and elite group of people. Their general name was "Believers", but their sub division was called "Etherians". They practiced a spiritual form known as "to catch you"! What they caught their pray in were "spiritual traps"! You see, they, by reading and gaining knowledge once applied become a form of wisdom; learned how to go form of wisdom: learned how to go from being spiritually hunted to being the hunters. Now at the time there was another group whom went into the hunters' jungle; but that was not them. They, the Etherians waited until certain soul hunters came after them as they did all men at the time. Only The Etherians did not desire as their main focus to" cast out", but to catch and mark. This way they could accumulate great scores in something called The Afterworld. They believed that Earth was part of an underworld, a place of suffering for transgression passed down from ancients long ago. And it was during a period called life, or the flesh prison that they had to due their work to prepare for "the first death" or transmutation into one of two general other worlds of existence forever. They had to gather and acquire specialized tools and learn how to use them. And they learned how to set something called Meta Traps. Often while learning they stayed hidden due to their value if caught unready. Day and night for years they made ready themselves. And once the game began, they would do something called "to unleash the dogs". I know it sounds strange, but they believed that the Lord favored his champions. They believed in a Book of Remembrance. They believed that the Lord had special people on standby to do his work. They wanted to feel and use the Power of The Lord! They often reflected upon great warriors of The Lord. They also studied how these, The Lords people were approached and led into something called "Sin"! Often times they would take on the responsibility to try to prepare their families, although it generally didn't work. One of the key elements to The Etherians was to place letters and words in their minds. They believed that the mind was also a battlefield. They also believed that the spirit had the ability to recall, once it was free from the flesh, upon the spiritual plane or after life. And once they became strong on the spirit plane, they were usually tested to the maximus. Once their degree of spiritual eutheric power was known, generally they were left unbothered due to their expertise. The negative soul catchers rather for them to be in their tempting flesh form rather than their immutable body. The reason being their mind intention upon the spiritual plane, and their found favor with The Lord. As a matter of fact, a great deal of their knowledge came from that which is written, but must be understood, about The Lord! And so, this Meta guy told me about a certain individual whom enjoyed to pervert men's wives and women. I was told about the ways of a very tricky entity. I heard of how it enjoyed saying in round about ways that The Lord was and is a liar! Then I was taught certain techniques just in case if I ever ran across this type of animal. But I thought why should I ever, ever, ever see such a thing? Meta said, yes my friend I thought the same exact thing. Plus he added that he was bewildered to find out who it and they were! I asked him about that, and he responded with something about from time to time becoming "The Angry Clown" in the spiritual world. I asked weren't clowns suppose to be funny? He laughed and said "they are, they are real funny, you won't believe how funny" and especially when they start tripping, what ever that means! Then Meta gave me this note that says "In The Day, Remember, Before The Life, Remember After The 1,000 Years, Remember, Guess Who Was Released In Great Anger Upon The Earth, But Will Be Cast Down Again? Second question, guess who perverted the wife of someone created "he, her, them"? Third question, of who can you use the Euthrian Form upon because although it stands upright now, in the book you read The Lord God Broke his back? Last question. Ah, what is another name for being angry; hint: Mad AQ Anagram: Who has your wife Vee? Open to find out? "So when Adam opened the note, he saw written real big, "Be Quiet!" "You Are Looking And Talking To What You Think Is A Snake, But Remember, You Adam, Which Is Mad A Spelled Backwards, Named The Animals, And Why Is Vee, Which Is A Anagram Of Eve Standing Beside The Serpent Master Of The Craft Of Deception, Illusion, And Disguise In The Form Of A Snake? Look Euthrian Style, he has taken your wife, and plus she wanted to go! Bonus Maximus Points Meta. P.S. Don't forget to involve the name as you recite the charges!" And so, with what is called The Quickness, Adam reached out and grabbed the serpent by the throat and called out The Invocation. And Adam went Eutherian upon The Serpent until you know who got their. The rest is a mad angry clown business Yelp! I hope you enjoyed it, and it expanded your mind. Know yee not The Scriptures? P.S. I wonder if this may be a source of what I have heard to be happening when it rains but the sun is out? Go Adam!

CHRISTIAN KABBALAH

See, Look: and so you have gone elsewhere? First, have you read The Bible from cover to cover? Have you researched "all" the words, not names, that you don't understand? Have you gone to ponder Revelations 13:18? Go back now! Look up all the verses of The Scriptures? P.S. I wonder if this may be a source of what I have heard to be happening when it rains but the sun is out? Go Adam! The Invocation. And Adam went Etherian upon The Serpent until you know who got their. The rest is a Mad Angry Clown Business. Yelp! I hope you enjoyed it, and it expanded your mind. Know yee not Meta. P.S. Don't forget to invoke The Name As you Recite The Charges!" And so, with what is called The Quickness, Adam reached out and grabbed the serpent by the throat and called out beside the serpent, Master of The Craft of Deception, Illusion, and Disguise in the form of a snake? Look Adam, Etherian style, he has taken your wife, and plus she wanted to go! Bonus Maximus Points.

ETHERIC ANKH

There is a symbol that I do not see among the Egyptian collection that is very important. It is the image of a man sitting with ankh coming from his phallus area. This is implying that the sexual center, or mystical seed is activated which is called having been fully charged <ether-ic>. Now in the sequence of the seeds' movement; it could be at the base of the spine, or in motion towards the pineal gland <pineal body: a small usually conical appendage of the brain of most vertebrates that has an eyelike structure in reptiles and functions in time measurement in some birds <source: Merriam Webster's High School Dictionary 1996>> which is located in the head. The mystical seed is like a particle of radiation that feeds the human body with electromagnetic radiation. The general concept is that the seed has enough charge to grow the one human body, while the human must till "the earth" to recharge the seed to grow the second spiritual body. The seed might be thought of as a rechargeable battery of the two bodies.

<Kundalini is not a life force by itself. It is a particular passage for the life force-a way....The kundalini and its chakras (centers) are not located in the physical body....The passage is in the etheric body and the centers also <NFR:JW218>.> <the seventh chakra, properly speaking, is not a chakra at all. It is often pictured in literature as a thousand-petaled lotus, he says, because it is actually the entire cerebral cortex with all its convolutions. He also maintains that the "opening of the third eye" is an expression referring not to the sixth chakra or some specific organ in the brain, but rather to the transformation of the entire brain and nervous system, with a resultant higher mode of perception <NFR:JW219>.> \

EGYPTIAN MINDSET

It is known that the Egyptians had a different way of thinking due to the religious writings found. The problem has been in trying to understand what they were talking about. I would like to explain one of the major concepts. The Egyptians knew that everyone in general would die in this physical world. Why would they build great temples for the dead? You have to remember that in The Bible Egypt was active until the time of Moses. Now according to The Bible, Moses lived long before Jesus The Christ. According to The Bible, the coming of Jesus also brought the first resurrection of the dead. Notice that Moses and Elijah were seen with Jesus at The Transfiguration. Someone asked Jesus how could a man be born again? What was implied was the question of how can a full-grown man enter into this world coming through the womb of a woman. This issue shows that the people of Jesus' day had a hard time understanding the spiritual concepts. The question is what is this rebirth? In the Egyptian mindset, man was not one person but two. One self was called the Ka, the other self was called the Ba. The two selves were connected to the earth body. So if we imagine the flesh as the earth body, then we can think of the Ka as the mind or conscience. Now the mind lived inside of the human brain. As you know, when the human body dies, the brain also dies. The brain is the general area that the mind lives in. To the Egyptians, the mind came and left the brain often. An example of this would be during times of sleep. The Egyptians believed that the mind could travel during sleep or meditation times. This is where you get astroprojection from. They even believed that the mind could travel around planet earth and view current events. Instead of taking an airplane to China, one might project the mind to visit the country. After the visit to China, the mind would come back to the brain. Upon waking, the person who went mentally to China could tell others what was happening in China. This is also the source of what is called a ghost or spirit, but in this case the body is dead. Now due to the use of the will, the mind stays upon the earth plane. Because the mind knows what the physical form looks like, the mind could generate a form that could be detected in the physical by the human eye. Now could that be possible? You have to remember that the mind is thought to have energy. Some levels of energy can be seen by the human mind. So the body of a ghost was really thought to be an energy signature or form of the mind of that which is the ghost. You could think of it like this. The mind and the Ka live inside of the flesh body. When the flesh body dies, the mind and the Ka were suppose to leave the earth physical plane and go to unite with the Ba body in another dimension The ghost is someone whom by use of the will decided not to move on but to stay upon the earth plane. 11-16-06

EGYPTIAN STASH

Once The Mind left the dead human body, The Mind would join with the second body The Ka. I should say that I have read that sometimes The Mind would hover around the dead human form for up to three days in usual situations. The Mind and The Ka would travel to another dimension where it would join with The Ba body. At this point the three would become as one. This was very important. Think of The Ba body as a spiritual bank account. The Ba body was a record of the value of the deeds that had been done by The Ka body while it was upon the earth physical plane in the earth flesh body. This is important because while The Mind could forget it's "goods and evils", the Ba body was made of the sum of them. This concept can be found in The Bible where it says that a person should place their valuables in heaven where man can't steal them. Why? Because it is The Ba that was going to be weighed at the judgement. The Ba was going to be weighed against a feather. If The Ba weighted more than the feather, The Ba was said to have "gross matter" in it. Therefore The Ba would be rejected from going to "heaven". If The Ba failed the test, the three would fall into denser levels called Hell. If The Ba passed the test, the three would float up into The Heavens. This was thought of as the wind called The Word moving the three upon the mystical boat, feather, or magic carpet. Float on!

EGYPTIAN MARTIAL

I remember first reading about a strange energy that one could posse in 1976. I was reading a martial arts magazine. I had no idea of what the article was talking about. There were these high level Black Belts doing all kinds of unheard of things. Sometimes I would see some of the activities shown in movies. Then there was these Chinese Priest types doing all kinds of strange King Fu. Then I became aware of Yogi masters doing some pretty strange stuff. I came to realize that the common bond was work with The Ba or Etheric body. The knowledge of this was in Egypt. The writing of it is written upon the temple walls. Oh, I forgot to say that I remember that one of the people interviewed was asked how long did it take to learn some of those special abilities. He said that with special training it would take maybe twenty years. Twenty years, I won't even go into how the energy structure of The Ka may be in a state of "brown out" if it is related to my current kundalini energy figures related to the earth's harmonic frequency grid.

IN AFRICAN EGYPT

This is not how it was in Egypt Africa. Temple learning was not like what we do today. Temple learning was about unfoldment and presenting yourself. There were many temples in Africa. In each temple you learned a different skill. All day long your path of learning and life, you had to present yourself. You had to come forward, among your people to show how you had improved yourself. If you were found slacking, guess who might be the first one to "take you out"? Your mother! Yes she would be very hard upon you. Don't ask me why, even though I think I know; but that was how it was. All learning came from The Temples from which you now get the industrial revaluation idea of school. Thousands of years ago you had to present yourself. It was a grand party.

GRAND PARTY

Yes during the day you saw your teachers in regular form or dress. But at the temple assembly, they dressed and looked strange. Their ware and station showed their rank. Now at the temple opening many strange happenings would be going on.

TEMPLES ON

You see, there were very many temples. In the houses of learning there are many schools. But at university, there was only one. It appears that in Egypt it was the mystical house of light. You might know it as The Great Pyramid. The place of The Great Fire. But as the master moved up and came towards it, they became more humble as they walked the path of life. The thought that they were looking into the stone face of infinity. A great many of times the temple ceremonies were two fold. The first being an introduction of a new member or player, the second being a master stating they are ready to be tested against the great unknown. That is the great test of the masters. To be tested in ways that are not heard or known of. To see if one can adapt to a new unknown environment! Now that is a test. That was Africa. Yes all of the known arts were known there. Music, math, body movements, animal natures, earth science, herbs, etc. What had you studied? The scrolls called now scriptures! It all came out in The Temple. Today you might think of the action of the temple as a Disco, but this was a master's spiritual ritual jam. There was an end, and there was a mean!

TEMPLE FUNK

I'm gonna tell you what I know. From the way a person moves in certain environments you can tell. You just know and can feel things about their core. That was what the temple was about. You knew them, some how. How another human creature walked, moved, or danced. You could see them. Hidden in the darkness of the daylight, but in The Temple it was very hard to hide. If you could, you did; but if you were out of great step with the grand leader, The Pharaoh, of whom represented The Lord God; you would shine like a red light among the blue lights. It was the coming together of all of the knowledge of The Lords Land, Egypt! And hence the origin of all of the inner and outer temple knowledge. Present yourself. You could not hide. In Egypt, what a fool that thinks that they could hide from the light. Not The Light, but the is Light!

OH, THE TEMPLE ARTS

See, for you to understand that, you would have had to been raised up in a temple, or someone would have had to had taught you how to get pass the gates. Now why should I have, already done that? Study dear students! But can I ask "one" question? Of whom is "Metatron"! Figure out that and pi and we shall see?

LOGIC'S

There are many forms of logic. One form of human logic, when I was confronted with it made no sense to me. Spiritual logic means to consume the spiritual scriptures, which are of the 97th percent and above, and act upon them and what you calculate. You are trying to approach the 100 percent, even though that is mathematically impossible that is where you are going! Ride, it's a hard ride! But ride, and ride if you can. Only a few are said to be worth it! It could be you!

JUST MAYBE

Just maybe, just maybe; oh if I have made "a hard run", just maybe we will one day see! Just maybe. Pharaohcon! The best I can say is that It is a very angry clown. "Angry Clown"! Not very funny. You are going to have to present yourself!

AKANOTENS EGYPTIAN GNOSTIC VISION:

THEORY OF THE IMMUTABLE KUNDALINI

PARTICLE SEED SYSTEM IN MAN &

"ETERNAL EGYPT":

MASTERWORKS OF ANCIENT ART

FROM THE BRITISH MUSEUM

CIPHER PART ONE

DEAR CURATOR OF THE BRITISH MUSEUM

AND

THE AMERICAN FEDERATION OF ARTS

BY
FRANK M. CONAWAY, JR.

WORKS

Works: 7-20-04 Book 1: **THE IMMUTABLE KUNDALINI PARTICLE SEED SYSTEM IN MAN & ETERNAL EGYPT CIPHER PART ONE**

<><1 >	Done Akanoten's Vision Cover
<><2 / 3 >	Dear Egyptologist From Egypt: Akanoten's Vision / Dear Curator (under doneemailcuratorletter4)
<><4 >	Osiris Phallus
<><5 >	Egyptian Fun House
<><6 >	Egyptian Put Out
<><7 >	Etheric Ankh
<><8 >	The Battle Of The Two Yous
<><9 >	From Nothing
<><10 >	What Is Hell?
<><11 >	Dimensions
<><12 >	See The EMF
<><13 >	In Egypt
<><14 >	Pi Lie
<><15 >	The Bozo

<><16 > Fronter

<><17> Night Right

<><18 > Dumb

<><19 > Spiritual Verses Manic

<><20 > Hidden Genesis Code

{Dear Egyptologists,

If you would please take the time, would you please review my discovery about the Eternal Egypt exhibit. Please send me your valued comments, as I am about to publish in an effort to receive degree. Your help is greatly valued, and forwards are welcomed. Thank you, Frank Jr. .}

March 22, 2004

From:
Frank M. Conaway, Jr.

To:

Walters Art Museum
Baltimore, Md
Atten: Curator

Dear Curator,

I had the pleasure of enjoying the "Eternal Egypt" exhibit at your museum. I purchased a copy of the catalog. In reading the catalog, I noticed on page 28 the statement: "there are two significant barriers to our engagement with Egyptian art. The first barrier is inadequate knowledge. Even among scholars, this ignorance encompasses not only basic questions about the dates of some of the works, but also larger and more persuasive uncertainties about meaning, purpose, and function. We do know that almost all Egyptian art was in some sense religious."

In response to that statement, I would like to submit to you, for review, a metaphysical cipher of several items shown in the catalog. I have only included in this package of a few of the pieces that I have worked on. I thank you for your time and consideration.

Sincerely,
Frank M. Conaway, Jr.

From Eternal Egypt: Akhenaten's Vision

A metaphysical cipher of the “Masterworks of Ancient Art From The British Museum” from the “Eternal Egypt” exhibit by Frank M. Conaway, Jr. author of “Baptist Gnostic Christian Eubonic Kundalinion Spiritual Ki Do Hermeneutic Metaphysics“ ISBN # 0-595-20678-6 copy written 2001.

“Eternal Egypt features a selection of the most important and beautiful objects from ancient Egypt, a civilization of enduring fascination. Written by Edna R. Russmann, with contributions by a distinguished team of international scholars, the lively text examines over 140 works and highlights the extraordinary artistic achievement that they represent. The book is published in conjunction with a traveling exhibition organized by the American Federation of Arts and The British Museum and drawn exclusively from the collection of the British Museum, which is among the finest in the world. Lavishly illustrated with images of the works in the exhibition, as well as comparative materials, Eternal Egypt is that rare book of interest and value to the general and scholarly audience alike.” <From the rear cover.>.

It is well known that the Egyptians were well concerned with what is called “a life after death” <ka: an aspect of the personality or soul that was born with a person and survived after death; it could receive offerings for the deceased. Sometimes represented as a twin image of a person, the ka was a kind of life force. Kings and gods also had kas. <Eternal Egypt: Page 264>>. The first point I would like to make is the relationship between The Bible and ancient religious system of Egypt. The Bible states that Moses was a master of all the Egyptian arts. Sigmund Freud is known to some as being the author of “Moses And Monotheism”. I refer to this so that right up front the readers will realize that a great deal of information is being discussed by the intellectuals that has not reached the general public. Before I discuss a whole or complete science of Egyptian philosophy <not included>, I would like to discuss certain, and not all, elements of various pieces of work from “Eternal Egypt”.

1) <The cover:> On the cover of the “Eternal Egypt”, notice the serpent on the headdress of the statute. In the hidden biblical

science this relates to the rising of the serpent power of the spine into the head, or more accurately into the pineal gland. This activates the unfolding of the mystical flame letters of that called the ancient holy texts <Including the “Pyramid Texts” <Eternal Egypt: Page 266>>.

2) <The rear cover:> Notice the crown upon the headdress of the statute. There are three elements. The two elements are the golden arches, which imply the two tablets of The Ten Commandments. Using the science of the Kundalini <The Serpent-coil (speirema) 200 + 80 + 5 + 10 + 100 + 8 + 40 + 1 = 444><spermaceti: a white, waxy substance obtained from the head of the sperm whale. <NFR>> system, one tablet would stabilize Ida and the other Pingala. Yes, the two tablets have different words or values upon them. In a mathematical sense, this is very accurate. Why? Because one side of the body <in the Pythagorian school of thought> relates to pi, and the other relates to phi. Using the musical mathematical science of binaural beat induction upon the three main cords of the human body <the left side, the right side, and the center path associated with the spine>, one needs to stabilize the left side of the body with the right side. The mathematical formula for this could be thought of as: pi X equals phi, or phi X equals pi, or pi X phi Y equals zero. That zero would cause a standing wave situation in the spinal column thus allowing the unification of the left and right sides of the brain. Hence, if thy eye <of the mind or brain> be as one. Notice the solar disk of Ra <Re equals Raa, because in one system of converting or cipher, AA equals E, AAA equals or can be unified as I, and so on.> <As another side note: Ra being converted into Raa or Re implies that the “a” in Ra is an alpha or large “a” in power.>. This represents the mystical seed said to be written upon with “The Law“ within man. This seed is what lays dormant in the human Ark of the Covenant. The seed needs the mystical waters of life to come to full power. It should be said that the mystical seed requires a few things. It must be watered with the waters of life. It must be given the correct spin, the seed being or making a sphere. It must be released from the lower chamber of the spinal system and raised in to the mystical upper chamber of the mind. Notice the staff in the statue's

hand. This implies the Kundalini system, and to make the spinal path straight. It also refers to the ancient riddle of the Sphinx <Notes from research: source not given but acknowledged equals <NFR>> <sphinx: a fabled monster having the head of a woman and the body of a lioness. <NFR>> <dragon: a fierce, violent person, male or female; a spiteful, watchful woman; a short carbine, carried by the original dragoons. <NFR>> <draconian [From Draco an Athenian lawmaker.] Harsh: rigorous. <NFR>>: "Tunnels under the Sphinx. Over the years, the Sphinx has revealed some of its secrets, though not all. In 1881 Henry Vyse found two tunnels inside the Sphinx, but his discovery was never published. In 1979, we opened these tunnels. The first tunnel is located behind the head of the Sphinx, cut into the mother rock about 6 meters. The second tunnel is located in the tale of the sphinx. We learned of it from Sheikh Mohamed Abd al-Maugud, who in turn knew of it from his grandfather. It too is cut into the mother rock about 12 meters. We found no significant artifacts inside the tunnel, but the evidence suggests that the tunnels were cut during the pharaonic period, I believe during the Twenty-sixth Dynasty. A third tunnel, in the north side of the Sphinx, has not been opened since 1926, when Emily Baraize opened it. We have photographs showing two workmen inside it." "That weathering of the Member II layers indicates that the Sphinx was built between 5000 and 7000 BC." "When Napoleon came to Egypt in 1798, the Sphinx was completely covered with sand. Napoleon's expedition mapped the Giza plateau and cleared the area around the Sphinx's head and neck to take measurements." "Caviglia concentrated his work between the paws of the Sphinx <Bastet <Eternal Egypt: Page 262>> <sphinx: The body of a recumbent lion with the head of a king or, less often, a royal woman; a manifestation of royal might, first appearing in the 4th Dynasty. In one variant form, only the royal face is shown, framed by the lion's mane and ears; on other sphinxes, the lion's forelegs are replaced by human arms and hands, which usually hold offering vessels. <Eternal Egypt: Page 267>> and found the so-called dream stela and fragments of the Sphinx's beard, one of which is kept in the British Museum, the others in the Cairo Museum."

"Auguste Mariette started to clear the sand around the Sphinx in 1853, then switched work to the lower temple of Khafre, before returning to excavate the Sphinx in 1858. He cleared the sand until he reached the Sphinx floor, found the protective wall left in the north side by Thutmose IV, cleared the shaft on the Sphinx's back and, finally, found the masonry blocks that were located on the sides of the Sphinx. Based on a statue base of Osiris, he believed that a number of large masonry "boxes" located on the north and south of the Sphinx were chapels for Osiris, and dated them to the New Kingdom." <NFR: ZH> <Notice 6 meters and 12 <6 plus 6> meters. <From the Holy Bible: Revelation: 13:18 Here is wisdom. Let him that hath understanding count the number of the beast: for it is the number of a man; and his number is Six hundred threescore and six. Another interpretation puts it this way: Here is cleverness (sophia): he who has the Nous, let him count the number of the Beast; for it is the number of a man, and his number is 666.> <According to the Gnostic cipher key, the riddle of 666 is answered by the Greek term for "Hephren <8 + 500 + 100 + 8 + 50 = 666>". Hephren means the lower mind. <NFR:JMP/JW> <The ego>> What goes on all fours in the morning, on twos in the midday, and by three in the evening <Note: I heard of riddle on a Batman episode years ago> <Bat: an important early cow goddess. <Eternal Egypt: Page 262>>? The answer was given as "man". Well, that is one of the answers. I will not go into all of them now. But I will say this. The beast man goes on all fours <Sphinx?>. The mark of the beast <Revelation 13:11: And I beheld another beast coming out of the earth; and he had two horns like a lamb, and he spoke as a dragon.> being a core of six. <In the Apocalypse four animals-symbols or beasts (theria) are conspicuous dramatis persone: (1) a lamb (or "little Ram," arnion), having seven horns and seven eyes, and who is identified as Iesous <The Higher Mind (Iesous: 10 + 8 + 200 +70 + 400 + 200 = 888) <NFR: JMP/JW>> <Jesus [Gr. Iesous, ~ Heb. Yeshua, "help of Jehova] The founder of Christianity: also Christ, Jesus Christ, Je-sus of Naz-a-reth. Christian Science, the highest incarnation of the divine idea in human form.>, who becomes "the Conqueror" <ho nikon 70 + 50 + 10 +20 +800 +50 =

1,000 <NFR:JMP/JW>>; (2) a beast resembling a leopard, with a bear's feet and a lion's mouth, and having seven heads and ten horns; (3) a red dragon, having seven heads and ten horns, and who he is “the Devil and Satan”; and (4) a beast having two horns like a lamb but speaking like a dragon, and who is called the pseudo-seer, or false teacher (pseudo-prophetes). Of these four the leopard is particularly referred to as “the Beast” <NFR JMP/JW>>. Six times four equals twenty- four. Two plus four equals six. This implies the ignorance of the knowledge of the Living God and a belief in something called time. There seems to be two times. One time has to do with the motion of the planets. The other time is a variable relating to a person’s life span. The two is speaking of the two feet of the upright man <Note: In a system of two units as one, sometimes called Bipolar; the two as one may be shown as a hermaphrodite, androgynous, or having two sexes <The identity of Akhenaten’s figure is not in doubt: his names are written in the cartouches <cartouche: meaning of all that the sun encircles. <Eternal Egypt: Page 263>> before his face. The delicacy of the features and around breast, which prompted some early observers to suggest that it represents Nefertiti (whose name appears with Akhenaten’s in the framing inscription, are simply a softened version of his scrawny and strangely androgynous physique. Such details as the large, heavy-lidded eye suggest that this stela was made late in his reign. A date late in Akhenaten’s life may have also influenced his being represented with a short, round, curled wig, unusual for this ruler. The same headdress appears on several later representations of his father, Amenhotep III, where the intent was clearly to identify the old king with the child god, Neferhotep <As in Nefertem, who is defined under the term Path <Eternal Egypt: Page 266>>, as part of his self-deification program. Neferhotep, part of the pantheon that Akhenaten had repudiated, would not have been acceptable. But the iconography of the juvenile god may well have appealed to this aging son of the Aten. <Eternal Egypt: Page 144>>. This can bring up the question of whether or not Adam of The Bible was created as he, her, them <Genesis 1:27>. This would be before the removal of Eve.> The three was said to be man in his old age using a cane. But in the mystical religious sense, it implies man leaning upon the risen God of the wood upright or cross <The Cross (stauros) 6 + 1 +400 + 100 +70 + 200 = 777 <NFR: JMP/JW>>. Remember, Moses had a rod or staff.

3) <Page 2> Although broken, you can see the remains of a form of a knot upon the headdress. This implies the threefold serpent system acting as one. The central serpent path being the dominant one.
4) <Page 6> How strange, an animal playing a board game <senet game <Eternal Egypt: Page 267>>. The animal resembles a horned donkey or goat. Recall the talking Mr. Ed. In the Bible, a donkey did talk and Jesus rode one. But what about the horns <Khnum: A ram-headed god whose main temple was on Elephantine Island at Aswan. As the creator of the human body and it's ka, he is often shown molding them on a potter's wheel. <Eternal Egypt: Page 264>>? In the Kundalini system, the two raised horns represent the activated Ida and Pingala. In the zodiac system, the horns would represent either Taurus or Capricorn. Capricorn being in December, who might this imply? Notice the X under the seat. This implies the crossing or source of the two lower currents. These are sometimes called rivers that flow from the spinal power source. And you know there were two sticks in the Ark of the Covenant. One called a rod and the other a staff. This implies that the two sticks were different some way.
5) <Page 16> In the lower portion, notice the two figures facing the same direction implying the union of the two into one power. The middle scene shows a pinhead pulling upward the hair, or etheric power of one like himself. The club <sekhem scepter <Eternal Egypt: Page 267>> is called the reed of power, the mystical bulb, the staff of power, or the spinal force. The bird scene is the mystical Phoenix performing the ritual of "The Opening of the Mouth" <sed festival, sometimes translated "jubilee" <Eternal Egypt: Page 267>> or central path of the flesh self <ego> that contains the six flowers <lotus, blue <Eternal Egypt: Page 265>> or chakras. Notice the body being shaped like a loaf of bread. So where is the seventh chakra? It is the bird who is activating his own colors or aura. The two figures with the horns represent Ida and Pingala.

6) <Page 17> Some things are strange, but some would say they are synchronicity. But use a piece of paper to connect the tops of the two pyramids. Notice the lines cross The Sphinx at the nose. I just added this due to the stated Kundalini systems use of the nose or breathing patterns to activate the mystical seed.
7) <Page 20> Noticed the statue has three elements. Two figures of lesser size, and one figure of a larger size. Notice the woman figure it is seated, while the male is standing, While the two seem to be in different positions, they represent the matured or raised Ida and Pingala powers of the central figure or body they are holding on to. The complete statue represents the active powers in the central body.
8) <Page 21> The headdress implies the raised serpent power. What is interesting about the two jars is that they appear to be equal. Each jar being different would represent the containers for the two different forces of Ida and Pingala. The hole in the center of the headdress is where the serpent power comes into the forehead. <Side note: you need another lover like you need a hole <whole> in your head> Also, the union of the two different spheres by the central core would imply the infinity symbol or the yin and yang sign.
9) <Page 22> On the standing statue notice the “coiled” <kundal: which means “a coil of the beloved’s hair.” <NFR: JW>> <The spiraling electrical force, “the coil of the serpent,” is the speirema, which word gives the number 444. Now, the action of this force upon the brain, where its triple current forms the cross, gives the noetic perception, direct cognition (the episteme, or highest degree of knowledge, so beautifully defined by Plato), and to express this in the diagram it becomes necessary to insert the word epistemon <Intuitively Wise: 5 + 80 + 10 + 6 + 8 + 40 + 800 + 50 = 999>, the philosophic equivalent for the word christos; its numerical value is 999. Further, he who has attained to this higher knowledge forthwith becomes the conqueror, and as “the Conqueror” is the hero, so to say, of the Apocalyptic Drama, his name must be placed at the head of the list, as ho nikon, with its number, 1,000. <NFR: JMP/JW>> object extending from the frontal source of the phallus <An image of the male reproductive organ, symbolizing in certain ancient religious systems the generative

power in nature, especially that carried in procession in ancient festivals of Dionysus or Bacchus. Anatomy: the penis or clitoris. <NFR>> <Bacchus: Mythology: In ancient Greece and Rome, the god of wine; Dionysus. <NFR>> power center on the front of the garment. Notice the two serpents. Up the center of the garment you see seven squares or rectangles <two squares>. They represent the seven system light centers in physics called ROYGBIV or VIBGYOR <Red, Orange, Yellow, Green, Blue, Indigo, and Violet>. You might even conclude that after the serpent power is raised from the lower sexual organ, it pierces the body in the side. This implies the jump of electromagnetic current <bipolar- a. light, electric motion b. magnetic, chemical induction> from the sexual organ into the low spinal column. Even the headdress implies seven motions <two at the neck, two at the ears, two at the temples, and one in the upper chamber of the head>.

10) <Page 23> The Façade of Great Temple. Notice the different size statues at the base of each seated figure. One might say that the seated figures represent the four comers of The Great Pyramid. They somewhat "appear" to be the same. The same can be said about the human body. From one comes five. From the four seated figures comes the hawk <Phoenix> headed one with the solar disk or sun. Notice the figures rest inside of an unequal sided square. Notice the figures on each side of the hawk figure. Again Ida and Pingala are raising up the central path power of the mystical immutable seed. At this point I would like to introduce the concept of the vertical coffer. A coffer could be called a chest or treasury. We shall see this concept later, but I will say it has to do with the immutable seed being raised through the seven <ROYGBIV> power centers. The seed makes a ninety degree rotation at the necks power center to stand the mystical seed <which charges the immutable body> upright <akh: the transfigured one; an aspect of the soul <Eternal Egypt: Page 262>>.

11) <Page 25> I would like to say something about the slanting or oblong of the eyes. This implies what the ancients say about the Kundalini force as it fires through the pituitary gland into the pineal center <called the Black dot>. The ancients say that once the pituitary gland beings to become

saturated, sparkles of light emit from the sides of the eyes <Egyptian Blue <Eternal Egypt: Page 263>> <When it moves through the chakras, the kundalini burns like fire through the channels or nerve currents which carry it upward to the magnetic part of the mind and brain. Strictly speaking, what is burning and moving is not a chemical or an energy; but energy is the byproduct, just as light is completely unquantized until it is absorbed or impinges on something resulting in the release of heat and energy as a byproduct. So is consciousness the same as unquantized light. Only when it moves through the system can it be described as kundalini because only then do we become conscious of its existence as an ambrosia which melts and burns. <NFR: JW>>. Also counting the horizontal lines in the headdress, it appears to be seven. The left and right sides are the two houses or pyramids; then the third or great pyramid extends from the base of the neck on each side to the top of the head. The serpent <which is missing> raises out of the coffer and appears into and through the mystical upper chamber of the mental pyramid or mind.

12) <Page 27> Animal Fable: The story is about three animals. The standing animal is saying that the body of the bird is dead, but here are its seven feathers raised upon a staff to represent the ankh sign of life. The chaired or seated being <animal> is sitting upon the box or ark of life. Noticed the "X" marking the spot. In one hand he holds a scepter or spinal representation, while in the other he holds a cup or bowl of life giving fluid. And yes while the body or flesh of the bird <Phoenix> is dead, the power or mystical seed is in the box. Noticed the horn or triangle upon the seated beings head. Now notice how the tail makes the rear enclosure of the box. So if the seated being stands up? But how? By the mystical words upon the scroll in the standing animals hand. The question is can the standing animal read, or "know ye not the scriptures".

13) <Page 28> The Mirror Handle: This is strange. Paragraph two starts with: "the first barrier is inadequate knowledge. Even among scholars, this ignorance encompasses not only basic questions about the dates of some works, but also larger and

more persuasive uncertainties about meaning, purpose, and function. We do know that almost all the Egyptian art was in some sense religious:". To me, the question seems to be rather or not you understand the Egyptian religion! Of this piece I would like to comment upon the woman holding the kitten <a play upon lion> aspect. Notice the name Kundalini. Kundalini is the name of the science, but in its singular internal aspect it is called: Kundalion. This Kundalion force <in males> is said to be the feminine aspect of the original seed of life from the sperm and egg process. The lion is the great guardian of the seed resting in the body. That which guards your original sperm seed. That one seed sperm that entered into the <red dot <rising sun>> egg and became you. The first cell of you! The one half a billion to one sperm and the bulls eye egg. A lion is a grown cat or large kitten. And who rulers the jungle after man? But is Egypt in a jungle?

14) <Page 29> Stela of Wep-em-nefret: One day, and I remember that day, it came to me one way the images from the Egyptian Wall could be read. Let me start with the nine glyphs over the seated mans head. One way to think of this scene is that the man seated upon the chair of beast legs wants the object of his external eye. He wants that which is in the container, the water of life. The black dot <In the Coptic language itself, the late written form of the ancient Egyptian, "Egypt" is designated by chemi, literally "the black land" (from chmom, "black"), probably referring to the rich black silt of the Nile, and "Egyptian" is remnchemi, "person of Egypt. <NFR:GG>> is the half or less than fully charged pineal gland <third> "eye". The black mound represents the iris of the eye, which is the horizontal eye <pituitary gland <pit>> inside the head. If he were to look within, or behind himself <the flesh being the outer image of the self>, then he would see that which sees from behind himself. With the will of his own mind, he would move the <pineal> black dot into the open <pituitary gland> eye, causing the eye to see, or elongate. This would knock over the instrument <stringed <Ida and Pingala>> making the mystical tone. The tone would cause the bird <Phoenix> to fly into the mystical horns <raised and balanced Ida and Pingala>. The horned birds

wings would sound the mystical flute <of the chakras <chi, ka, ra>> bringing into birth the reborn bird <Phoenix>, which becomes the new head upon the shoulders. Due to the new life, the hand raises and the sound of one hand clapping is heard. This one hand opens the mystical door <pyramid>. Once the hand raises or is opened, if it closes down, the door <false door <Eternal Egypt: Page 263>> closes under it <or as the Kundalini force in the pituitary gland <the crescent moon power> charges the solar <pineal> center, the mystical opening of the mouth happens. As the cup that holds the water of life fills, the seated man will be able to drink from it through "a straw" or reed! Notice on the table are eight feathers. Yes, but between them are seven lines or cells as in a battery. These represent the seven <ROYGBIV> <chakras> phases of light within the darkness of the body.

15) <Page 30> Temple of Amun: The image deals with the raising of the Kings scepter. The mini lower selves, including the central two <Ida and Pingala> are being raised or drawn up by the central shaft, pole, or cord. Notice the mystic rainbow coming from the cup around the reed, staff, or tree <palm, hand>. It could be said that the mystical waters from below are flowing <running over> from the above cup above. What is going to happen to the people below the cup? They are either going to be baptized or drowned from the ever flowing water.

16) <Page 31> Banquet Scene: The upper scene deals with the activation of the seated Ida and Pingala. Although they are being served by the mystical raised female <Kundalini>, they are being served or attended to by the mystical male seed. Look at the change in position of the bald headed one between the woman's arm. From the right, the first four images show the seated <dormant> <Ida and Pingala> being introduced to the young <fully charged> male scene. You know the standing woman is the superior and elder because of her showing pubic hair. The second scene shows the male <seed> touching Ida and Pingala <seated>. Noticed the open flower to the face. In the third scene, where is the young male <it is a moving picture>? The male seed has entered into Ida and Pingala. How? He split <bipolar>. Now the

three women are as one. Ida, Pingala, and the central shaft called Sushumna! Now in the lower scene, you still see the seated six ladies; but you also see Sushumna seeded with them. But look, there is the male again standing tall in front of another seated figure. He and the seated woman represent the union of the Kundalini force with the mystical seed <to be reborn through the mystical mother. Those things on the heads of the seeded women represent the mystical “tongues” of fire. In the Kundalini system it would represent the various stages of the activation of the “globes <chakras> of fire” in the inner mystical tree of life. Now look at the food on the second layer of the table. Look at the basket of grapes in the two scenes. The upper scene has the mystic seed, loaf, egg, or sack in front of it. The lower scene tells you that the women have been charged through the seed of the mystical mother by the exchange of the fluid of life. Notice the towel or loin cloth <longi: meaning long: adj. long-horned. <NFR>> and the cupped hand prevent spillage. As a note, a simple diagram of a simplified tree of life would have a triangle on top of a square, on top of another square, on top of an inverted triangle. Where the triangles meet the squares, put circles <globe, sphere, chakra> at the corners; and where the squares meet, put circles in the corners. This would make six circles. Draw a line from peak of one triangle to the peak of the next. Put a circle where each line crosses another line. This is the center path that the mystical seed ascends the spine. Put a circle at the peak of the lower triangle. This is the starting point of the Kundalini mystical rebirth. Put a circle at the top of the upper triangle. This is the upper chamber, or resting place of the risen mystical seed. But were does the seed come from? From the lower triangle. Below the lower sphere, draw a sphere at least one sphere and a little away <extend the centerline>. You should now have twelve spheres. But the twelfth sphere changes when it becomes activated, so in reality, one could say the twelfth seed is cut off from the tree, and a new seed takes its place. The thirteenth seed. Notice not only do the women have the “tongues of fire” upon their heads, they also have overturned bowls or eye forms.

18) <Page 33> Mycerinus: Figure nineteen has thirteen layers upon his "beard" <if you will>, while figure twenty only has nine. So? Figure nineteen has the raised serpent, while figure twenty does not. So? The nine levels refer to the three simple levels of Ida and Pingala, which equals six spheres. The other three levels equal the two spheres at the top of the triangles in our simple tree of life, and the "twelfth" sphere that is chargeable. That is our nine. So how do we go from nine to twelve, and where is the thirteenth sphere? Twelve minus nine equals three. The three spheres are those of the central vertical path called crossings. So where is the thirteenth sphere, or mystical seed. Oh, the mystical serpent <power> has been born. See the serpent upon the headdress. Plus can't you see it upon his face? Look, his beard has grown, he has a mustache, and see his eyebrows!
19) <Paged 34> Seated Statute: Oh, oh, I really like this one. This requires the very specialized skill called swag. It combines a high scientific process with an ancient form of meditation upon a given problem. Well, you start off by eliminating what you know <well, believe> cannot be an answer! Then guess based upon what to do know. This is the statute of the eager learned student. Soon he will be the teacher, for his hand is ready for the writing tool <or he has been using a lot of highlighters <joke>>. At his feet <covered with plastic> are what he has learned. His body has suffered for the sake of his mind. He is mentally "sexy". You know he is, and so does he! See, he has been seated while learning a long time! Oh swag? Swag is scientific wild ass guess!
20) <Page 35> Sesostris III <kind of a serious business look>
21) <Page 37> Amenhotep III: To me, this is a very beautiful type of artistic expression. Notice the coiling feature of the serpent. The body seems to be as wide as the holes in the spinal disk. Notice the eyes. One could think of them implying being mostly closed for inner meditation while being fully open, even expanded during the same process.
22) <Page 43> Standing Statute: I wanted to say something about this piece because of its feeling. Look in his hands. I could imagine he has just received the rod and staff award of the master student. Master of the upper and lower Nile

award. The <shepherd> Hook and Flail award of Osiris. Why he even has upon his head the cap or wig. If they are beads, they would be in many colors. He knows, to himself, he has achieved. Happy <Hapy: a fecundity god of the Nile who personified the life-renewing power of the annual inundation and the fertile black silt that it brings with it. He was usually represented as a fat man with a sagging belly and large, woman-light breast, carrying offerings and crowned with a clump of papyrus. <Eternal Egypt: Page 264>> is that man!

23) <Page 67> Plaque with Den Smiting an Easterner: <see page 30, plus:> If we start to talk about East and West, let us reason upon the mystical directions. The sun rises in the East and sets in the West. So the man of the West, the second <inner> man or body is slaying the first of the flesh. Look between the raised united hands, five points as one. This refers to the five points of man. Ok, what is the sixth point of man? The phallus. What is the seventh point of man? The raised phallus or obelisk! Then what happens? The seventh power is released inside the body as the phallus power is made vertical, which is the image of the tail at the rear of the spine. Then what happens? Well to be short, the activated seed moves upward along the Nile of the spine. The mystic "fish" swims upstream to the upper source of the "Nile" <the spine>. The two hands up are the hands or currents of Ida and Pingala. Notice the <ankh <cross> and the black dot. <A proper raising of the Kundalini is said to produce remarkable states of awareness. The first awareness of Kundalini's awakening is a sensation of warmth which grows from warmth to a burning heat. Each chakra pierced and opened brings a new experience, new power, and a new vision. Oftentimes strange sounds are heard. Individuals who have experienced Kundalini say it is beyond description. The phenomena associated with it very and include bizarre physical sensations and movements, pain, clairaudience, visions, brilliant lights, superlucidity, physical powers, ecstasy, bliss, and transcendence of self. Kundalini has been described as liquid fire and liquid light. The finial objective of Kundalini rising may take many years. It is achieved when the Kundalini, or serpent power, reaches the final chakra

point inside the skull. With a psychedelic explosion it is said to awaken a ten-thousand-petal lotus. This is a graphic way of describing complete cosmic consciousness and god-realization. Descriptions are vivid. Brilliant stars and flaming tongues are seen. <NFR:JPN>>

24) <Page 70> Seated Statue: What looks like a farming tool over the shoulder, might just be the tool <shown larger> for artificially opening the <Hood of Ra> mouth.

25) <Page 79> Standing Nude Woman: excerpt: "the symmetry of the woman's pose is broken by a slight turn of her head to her right. This was surely intentional. Most Egyptian statues show small asymmetries; for example, one eye is very often higher than the other. In part, these may have been due to ancient working methods, but they seem also to have been appreciated for their enlivening effect. On statues of the late Old Kingdom, noticeable asymmetry occurs too frequently to be accidental. In at least one case, it was carried to a striking extreme. The painting of the pubes on this figure leaves no doubt that it, like catalogue numbers 8-10, is nude. While it is rather surprising that some male tomb owners of the late Old Kingdom and First Intermediate Period chose to have tomb statues that represented them naked and thus deprived of the status indicators of their clothing, it seems astonishing that women of high social rank, during this period, sometimes did the same. For although women of ancient Egypt did not suffer the restrictions imposed on women in many other cultures, they were certainly subjected to strong dictates of property. It is true that status of women, particularly in Old Kingdom, frequently emphasize sexual characteristics veiled by an impossibly skintight dress; but the existence of that dress is seldom in doubt. Yes this anonymous statuette, along with catalog number 10 and perhaps a dozen more wooden figures of nude females, very probably represents a high-ranking woman. The great majority of those with known province came from women's tombs at provincial sites outside the Memphite Asypt, Sedment, Naga el Der <Negus, [Amharic for "king"] The title of the Emperor of Ethiopia <NFR>> <The uniting thread I referred to is the ubiquitous symbol of the serpent

and its affiliation to the masters and adepts of many of the world's spiritual traditions. Traditionally these diverse masters have been intimately connected with the snake, serpent or dragon and referred to by regional names denoting "serpent." They have been called snake Nagas ("snakes") in India, the Quetzlcoatls ("plumed serpents") in Mexico, the Djedhi ("snakes") in Egypt, the Adders ("snakes") in Britain, and the Lung ("dragons") in China, to name the few. Collectively they have been called the "Serpents of Wisdom" and associated with the worldwide network of spiritual adepts known as the Solar or Great White Brotherhood. <NFR: MAP>>. In some places, the use of nude female tomb statues may have continued into the early Middle Kingdom, by which time the statues of their male counterparts were once again clothed. Until recently, all statues of nude women were assumed to represent "concubines," placed into in tombs to serve the needs of male tomb-owners. We now know that their functions were more varied. The most blatantly sexual of them were fertility figures, deposited as votive offerings in hopes of a child. Some were found in tombs, but others have been found in houses, and many from the shrine or temple of a goddess. Other naked female figures appeared to be servant girls or dancers, whose nudity is undeniably suggestive but also a sign of their extreme youth. In the New Kingdom, most such representations, such as catalog number 81, a cosmetic vessel, and figure 14, a mirror handle, functioned as luxury items that were used by male or female owners before being deposited with them in the tomb." What is not realized is that the whole, and I do mean whole, and again whole concept of what the sexual organs were about was so different in Egypt. I dare ask: "who was running around having ejaculatory sexual encounters in Egypt?" Besides, ancient Egyptian knowledge stated that the sexual organs needed direct sunlight. As far as men went, just because you obtained an erection, that was not your clue to have intercourse or masturbate. This comment is leading into discussing the activation of the sexual seed and the use of what is called sexual kung. These were and are highly specific sexual exercises used alone or with a partner <male and female> to amplify ones internal energy by charging and discharging the euthric seed. I happen to call the basic set of exercises “The Chinabar <Chi on / in a bar> set”. I would like to say, the objective of “The Chinabar Set” is to activate the eutheric seed power in the male and <no, no, no; too much about the secrets of the Chinabar!>! Well, let me say this, I have heard some women speaking about glowing, What can be said is that the mystical Chinabar has the ability to light the bulbs <chakras> inside the female tree of life. The female loses the red seed <power from the red chakra> every cycle, so her stabilized lower color is orange. The raw male seed is said to be eutheric red, with his spinal base being orange. Think of it as the woman being orange over red, while the male is read over orange. Yes, it is said that the woman can have more sexual encounters than the man. It is often forgotten that while the woman is pregnant one term, how many is it that the man can impregnate. But, as the female seeded is dissipated during the rhythm method, what is the rate of dissipation and regeneration of the male seed?

26) <Page 83> Stela of Tjeti : What I would like to say about this is look at the giant triangle <pyramid> at his midsection. What about the hidden doorway of The Great Pyramid, and this at a doorway? Get it <a mystery school>? You see the triangle <pyramid>, but you cannot “tell” where the doorway is? What is so important about a doorway? How can you get in, if you cannot find the doorway? Could it be said that you know it not! You cannot raise the mystical seed, even if you do activate it, unless you can find the doorway to the Internal Tree of Life. All you can do with the activated seed is become sexually overworked <all the time>. In the Bible Jesus says: “I am The Door”. So if he does not know you? Now suppose you find the doorway. Do you have a key? Look at the two figures behind Tjeti. The upper one has no key! Why? Because he used the key to get in so he could move from the lower <portion of the> self into the upper self.

27) <Page 84> Offering Bearer <notice again from the tomb of Tjetji> excerpt: “The woman is an offering bearer-not a real individual but a generic type, whose sole function was to

provide food magically for the tomb-owner’s use in the Afterlife. With one hand she balances a basket of food on her head; with the other she holds a live duck <duck, duck, and a? <goose>><duck: linen or cotton cloth; a water fowl; a pet <NFR>> <duct: a tube or passage <NFR>> by the wings <wing: an organ of flight <NFR>>. Because the figure faces left, which is the subordinate direction in Egyptian two-dimensional art, there is a characteristic reversal in her hanging hand, which looks as if it is shown backwards. This indicates that, although she appears to us as to be holding the bird in her proper left hand, she is actually holding it in her right, which is the way the hand has been drawn. Left or right, the duck seems to be taking advantage of its position to administer an impudent jab at the woman's posterior.” In short, the duck is the mystical seed being raised up through the central path of power called the Sushumna, which brings the male she serves the mystical water of life <which can be said as coming from her head. The waters of external life we know come from the male, so it is only natural to say that the internal waters are female in origin. Hence, an origin of the saying that behind every good man was a good woman.>

28) <Page 90> Seated Statue: On this page are two images. The first is a statue with the arms crossed. The crossing point is at what is called the solar plexus. This is the said crossing of the mystical seed at the green chakra. It would indicate the unification and stabilization of the two powers or chi in the two arms <Ida and Pingala> at the second point or crossing of the internal tree of life. The image next to it has many dots in the skull “cap”. These dots represent the “Thousand Points of Light” that are said to emanate from the mystical center <pineal gland> when the Kundalini power is activated.

OSIRIS PHALLAS

Among great suffering and great stress, the ancients say can come great enlightenment In the drama of Osiris, his phallas comes up missing, Where is it? Eaten <a play on Aten> by a great sea monster. In the system that I use, this would be called the Kundalion. Now after our great kundalini sea monster eats the sacred member, it returns to the waters of life to fertilize them. This was represented by the empty coffer in the queens chamber of The Great Pyramid. The kundalion is thought of as being female. The kundalion being female, is activated by the male sexual energy. Her eutheric radiation then fertilizers the waters of life. You see the waters in the coffer in one of the Walters Art galleries Egyptian works.

EGYPTIAN FUN HOUSE

So you want to have fun in Egypt. Well you can pay your money and see all the sights. Walk up the pyramid and hang from a rope, let go and slide down the side of the pyramid into a pool of water. Aren't those sail boat sails? Yes and no. See the crew of the boats use those sails when they buy goods to carry them back to the ship. Herbs, flowers, skins, etc.. Sometimes they pull things up upon the boats in the sails. Maybe sail bundles full of bread. And those on guard at night might sleep upon the sail and call it a blanket. But one day, the wind blew too hard. Someone was at the wrong place at the right time. Yes, blown off the ship. But they grabbed a sail, and the parachute was invented. Next people began to jump off of the pyramids. Some people would even jump off at night. They were said to be daring the Devil <the lie of a task being called impossible>. What did you called a person who parachuted off a pyramid at night? Oh, he's a bat <the blind leap of faith> man. And while the pyramid was being built, you also had rooms or cubical type cubbyholes. The origin of the cell and project housing design. Use the checker board to layout your design. What happened if a cubit cell was built, but no filler mix was put in? It could be a bathtub, pool, or flower box. Hey you could put fish in there. Yes, and go fishing. You could cover an empty cubit with a sail and put bricks on the sides and you would have a nice tent. Somebody used more bricks then their weight. Due to this, the sail sagged and the hammock was invented. But then, someone filled the cells with water and jumped up and down upon the sail and yelled trampoline. All was fine until a heavy guy walked across the sail. The bricks gave way some, and the sail dipped down into the water. The guys feet got wet, so he walked off the sail. We think the priests heard someone remarked about walking on water, so they closed the cells down and ban that type of activity. It was said that the priest were so mad, that when they snatched the sail from over the cell, not a brick moved. This may have been the source of snatching the tablecloth off of a fully dressed table. And speaking of tablecloths, you better not stain a block with your lunch. So at lunch they put down a sail for you to eat upon. The source of lunch in the park with a tablecloth. They also found out you could slide the bricks across the dried concrete <See Book Four: Building: A Pyramid How?>. So they made games to help get the bricks up the pyramid. Here's your shuffleboard, hockey, croquet, billiards pool, and bowling. See; all and all, it's just another brick in the wall. Want to make a wish, say your wish over the brick. Walk your wish brick up the pyramid. Throw it in an empty cell. What did you wish for? To stop carrying bricks. Did something wrong? You might get sentenced to carry five hundred bricks to highest unfinished level of a pyramid. Ever heard of throwing bricks at the penitentiary. Somebody figured out you could slide the bricks down a slanted sail. They call it the red brick carpet. What they found was you could fill up a cell with mix after bricks were dropped in. Its like putting stones in your concrete. But since the brick is the same as the mix, it will all come out in the wash. Hey, want to slide down the pyramid into a pool of water? How much does it cost? One brick! Yes, would you like to have nice pretty Egyptian feet? Well, for one hour you dance to the music in the mud pit, then you carry a brick up the pyramid <this being symbolic of reflecting upon a time of your life>. You leave your brick on the upper most level, then you slide down <symbolic of the return to the fallen world: reincarnation>. The first water ride. The first sliding board. Watch the experts do tricks jumping off the diving <cubit> board. Yes, want to get your nails done? Carry two bricks to the nail salon on level eight. Want your hair braided, go to the hair salon on level ten. Take three bricks. Want to learn your ABCs, let's tie this brick <in a back pack> on your back and off to school you go. How many students? Fifty. Well, that's forty-nine bricks and one apple. But how are we going to learn how to write? You write on <clay> brick tablets with these reed pencils. The teacher checks your work and puts your tablets in a hollow cubit. While building the pyramid, you have people walk up and placed their clay tablets into the "air shafts". The tablet slides like dominos <domino: robe and hood for masking: as in a hermit: as in the tarot card system> down the air shaft into the coffer. Maybe your brick will float? You might put sand in the coffer box so that the bricks don't break, nor make a lot of noise! Then people stack the tablets or bricks in the brick break room. What about those slabs of stone across the ceiling in the pyramid? Not a problem. Pour a slab and wait for it to harden. Then cover the slab with sand. Then repeat the process. The sand acts like an expansion joint. Well, how do we pour the ceiling? Have the people bring buckets or baskets of sand from the beach. Do you mean desert? Whatever! Pour the sand into the air shafts to fill the room. Once the room is full, block the shafts. Now pour the sand in from above. Have the math class figure out how many buckets of sand are needed to fill the room. Then we can have a raffle. Guess how many buckets are needed to fill up this room with sand. Free raffle ticket for drawing, Well how do they get the ticket? When they go up the pyramid to get their raffle ticket from an official in the room, they also get to see the room they are guessing about. They pay with a break. Carry as many as you want. What are you going to do with the tickets after the drawing. We are going to have a barn fire! Wait, how do we get the sand up the pyramid anyway? Oh, on the day of the drawing everyone comes out to fill up buckets and carry them up the pyramid. The official keeps count of the total number of buckets used. What about church? Yes, the Rev. said that he wants to see everyone on the pyramid for service, and everyone must bring him a break. Well, suppose we wanted to go way out in clay, what can we say? All cups, forks, plates <throwing disk, and skeet> must be made of the special "clay" mix. Once you are fed, put your trash into the container. The pyramid hollow cubit trash container, the true origin of recycling.

EGYPTIAN PUT OUT

You must understand that you could be put out of Egypt. They did not play that. That is the willful breaking of the laws. It was required that each person knew the laws <all the laws and the penalty for breaking them><not like today!!!!!!!!!>. Furthermore, the handwriting was on the walls. It was the laws and beliefs that modern age people consider as Egyptian wall art. And if you did something worthy of you being put out, they would ask you to leave by force. First you would have to work to pay any debts off and to buy a donkey. Then they would take you to the very end of Egypt. They would tie you up, put a facemask on you, and sit you upon your donkey. This was their way of saying that you were spiritually dead! Then they would kick your donkey in the hind parts <origin of the term: kicking your ass>. And off you go!

ETHERIC ANKH

There is a symbol that I do not see among the Egyptian collection that is very important. It is the image of a man sitting with ankh coming from his phallus area. This is implying that the sexual center, or mystical seed is activated which is called having been fully charged <ether-ic>. Now in the sequence of the seeds' movement; it could be at the base of the spine, or in motion towards the pineal gland <pineal body: a small usually conical appendage of the brain of most vertebrates that has an eyelike structure in reptiles and functions in time measurement in some birds <source: Merriam Webster's High School Dictionary 1996>> which is located in the head. The mystical seed is like a particle of radiation that feeds the human body with electromagnetic radiation. The general concept is that the seed has enough charge to grow the one human body, while the human must till "the earth" to recharge the seed to grow the second spiritual body. The seed might be thought of as a rechargeable battery of the two bodies. <Kundalini is not a life force by itself. It is a particular passage for the life force-a way….The kundalini and its chakras (centers) are not located in the physical body….The passage is in the etheric

body and the centers also <NFR:JW218>.> <the seventh chakra, properly speaking, is not a chakra at all. It is often pictured in literature as a thousand-petaled lotus, he says, because it is actually the entire cerebral cortex with all its convolutions. He also maintains that the “opening of the third eye” is an expression referring not to the sixth chakra or some specific organ in the brain, but rather to the transformation of the entire brain and nervous system, with a resultant higher mode of perception <NFR:JW219>.>

THE BATTLE OF THE TWO YOUS

Little known to the earth self is the fact that a spiritual master seed resides inside the human body. This is what gives the sexual organs seeds there polarities power. This little self, or mini me, is the spiritual side of a coin so to speak, of which the other side is the worldly reflection. The flesh itself acting as the metal of the coin and helps the two sides keep their form. To the human, flesh is a protection device from the elements, which include negative spiritual influences. But the battle is in the mind. You could think of chakra centers as 666. The front openings connect in six. The rear openings connect in six. The central path connects in six. So how do we get, or get to rather the seventh chakra center. Depending on if one is ascending or descending. If ascending, the person uses the red chakra for fuel, like in a rocket, a pinball type of pattern is the course which the spiritual seed must take. The red fuel must first be amplified until the point of combustion or else, there is danger of the upper chakras falling into it and being consumed. And that's what happens when a persons soul descends, it falls from the heavens of the mind, into the brain, probably the fourth ventricle, and downward through the color spectrum until it reaches the super nova red chakra. Boom! An explosion, or merger, that upon death of the physical body, sends the red energy into a collection of red energy, like the lava burning within the earth. But it is said, that with ancient techniques, a person, while alive, can achieve the spiritual level called liberation. Then “Boom”, they send their soul self out into the ethers to wait at the "gates" of heaven. But generally speaking, the worldly mind must be convinced that the only chance of its existence is the birth of the spiritual self from what is called the immutable seed <atom, atomic particle><see The Bible: <immutable: # 276: Hbr 6:18> <carried over: metatithemi: to transpose, to transfer # 3346: Act 7:16, Gal 1:6, Hbr 7:12, Hbr 11:5, Jud 1:4> <seed: Hbr 11:18, 1Pe 1:23, 1Jo 3:9, Rev 12:17, Rom 9:29, Luke 20:28>>! The water of life must be gathered. But the problem is in convincing and controlling the worldly ego self to cooperate. You are asking the worldly ego self to commit the ultimate sacrifice of suicide <it is hard to convince the flesh of non flesh things, and why should the flesh care about things not of the flesh? Hum! Yes, and why should the sperm <semen, spermatozoa> care about things beyond the reality of the sperm?>. Your spiritual self has to convince the worldly self that what is called the world is the most complex, almost and too perfect matrix illusion ever known to man. The world is the real fake for real <stemming from the original lie <and hence teaching the principles of lying to Adam and Eve <And hence, the false belief that you can lie to God The Creator, or The Lord God, and they believe your lie, when they know / are The Truth> <So you learned to lie to yourself!> <No, but it gets worse, some of you have learned to call a lie the truth, then "Believe" it. A self brain washing> <No, but it gets worse. Some have learned to "hate" and "reject" The Lord!> <So says The Lord <The Bible>>. The world is and is not. The world is like hitting the ultimate lottery and going on vacation for twenty years in a foreign country. Home, where is home? However long it takes you to forget home, your starting place, the earth plane is it plus a few centuries more. You are born as twin. And because you are born into the earth plane, the twin most in tune to it takes control. Some call it the evil twin, but it is really in opposition to the good twin called truth. See, without the systems of exploitation, none of this earth plane makes any sense. How can you charge money for fruit that grows wild every year? Who can say they brought some land? From where? Why don't we have meters over our mouths to count and regulate the air we breathe? When you buy milk, how much of the profits does the cow get? What is the fee for sunlight? The sun gives off heat and light. You pay the electric and gas companies for the same thing don't you? Who does all the gold, silver, brass, iron, and copper really belong to since you dug them up? Did you ever think that Gods laws, like let the earth rest on the seventh year, is his form of declared taxation? What happens if you fail to pay your spiritual taxes? Can you get away? Can you rob God? What does it mean when a person invents thoughts and ways outside of Gods teaching? Is this not a biblical point explained in the scriptures? Can a donkey talk? Where there giants upon the face of the earth? Can a rock follow you as you walk? Why did the Lord God appear in human form? When? Oh, how about in Genesis 18:1? Did The Lord God speak to men and eat food? When? Oh, how about Genesis 18:1? Must a man carry his own cross? Has judgment really come to planet Earth 2000 years ago <repent, for the <your> end is near>? What do you believe? What do you know? How? How? How does the caterpillar turn into the butterfly? What is so special about the sea horse? Where is Hale-Bopp now <Everybody's Comet by Alan Hale: ISBN 0-944383-38-6>? When will it return? Was it ever here before? When? Please tell me, when? Comets come in cycles don't they? Was the year 2000 the millennium? Was it 2001 because there is no year zero, or does the point of time called zero represent the cosmic egg day of the birth of Christ? Could zero represent that funny strange star, which some call the ship that brought the news of heavenly glory to the world? Or do you really know what time it is if the current calculations say that now, 2004, is really 2010? If Jesus was born in the year named six BC, what time is it now? What does this have to do with the Mayan prophesy of 2012 A.D.? Wow, three years and counting! Are you ready? I mean; if it is, and not if it is not! But suppose it is? Has the world, as we know it, been naughty or nice? I'm just saying! I'm just asting <asking> !

FROM NOTHING

I just ask myself, how can the something of this world be created out of nothing? Then I said, that is the wrong assumption. This world was created first by the Word in a two fold <bipolar> process. The Word surrounded itself. In other words, the Word created a shell around itself, called its own reflection or particle shell. The shell was alive or in motion, as to was the particle, core, seed, or reflection. Due to the natural wisdom called universal constants in mathematics, the shell began to grow mathematically inwardly, while the core particle began to expand. The "nothing" or space was caught between the two living forces and crushed. The motion of the expanding two forces continue until the two forces intersect. As in a sphere within a sphere both growing towards each other with mathematical hands or tentacles that would not or did not hold until balance is achieved. At that moment, called balance, the growth energy locks and stops, but the inertia of the various mathematical constants motions create many inertia waves which act violently upon the compressed space called darkness, and causes the space or buffer area and placement to change. This movement in the buffer system generates by vacuum induction collapse of the stabilized interlocked universal constants. You could think of filling a volume with fluid to a compression rate of just below the point of shear. Now quickly compress the exterior so that the size of the interior of liquid is reduced. Add two times the amount of fluid, and quickly remove the exterior compression. The compressing from the outside is one force. The compressed liquid is another force. The introduction of the two times fluid is an additional force. When these elements try to stabilize by coming in conflict with each other, what do you have other then imploding exploiting expanding contracting motion. But if the skin or outer shell can expand, what would you have in the vacuum? You would have a continually mathematically pulsating environment. So is the Sun the center of the universe etc.? Well, for us it is. Nature is trying to show you variations of the same universal constants.

WHAT IS HELL?

Hell is like needing one drop of water to stay in your current state of being, and not being able to find that one drop of water. Biblically, names can be reduced to mathematical universal constants through the science of the expansion of the flame Hebrew letters known in the higher levels of The Kaballah

<kabbala, kabbalah, kabala, cabala, cabbala, cabbalah> science. Once the name is expanded, it can be likened to the DNA code each creature carries. This code, signature, or sign of nature works just fine in its current environment called life upon the planet earth <A Northwestern Wildcats Motto: A pledge "To Seek, To Find, And Not To Yield!" And so, I bore witness to it!>. And for whatever dimension this is called, the current scientists now say they have proof of higher dimensions. Now if we name the earth dimension as "b", we can name the higher dimensions the same way. But if we say a new mathematics is at the higher dimensions cores, then in a simple form, we can grasp an idea of our own mathematical transit through them. Let "b" for birth stand for this current dimension. Let the next four dimensions be "c", "d", "e", and "f". Now assign a universal constant to rule each such as pi, phi, e, and the square root of negative one. Now if we agree that numbers don't die, then we can move from this dimension to and through the next providing that our own DNA or numerical sequence can bond or agree with the higher dimension. What I am saying is that if in our current inner mathematical core code we have as subsets these four universal constants, then we can move, via our own subsets, through the dimension that rules each subset. What stops each name or code from bonding with the dimensions are the other portions of the code. But suppose your name or code only has the subsets pi and phi in it. When your name <code> reaches the phi dimension it cannot pass into the "e" dimension <"To Hell And Back" A documentary produced by Trinity Broadcasting Network and featuring eminent cardiologist Dr. Maurice Rawlings.>. At the same time, your "pi" subset has been stripped away when you passed through. So now your name consists of phi and some other elements that your complete sequence name had when you were in the "b" dimension. Of course you cannot bond with pure phi. But the motion of the greater phi dimension acting upon your lesser phi subset in your name will soon affect your whole sequence. Soon the mathematics of your sequence will start to yield, deflect, then sheer upon themselves. The sequence of your name, which is you, will be mulched and mulched until no motion or sequence is left. And this leaves only the remembrance or shadow self to tumble within the never ending mathematical dimensions. The shadow self then

becomes part of the fuel system trapped inside of a never ending mathematical system. This shadow self is the off balance that keeps the dimension going.

DIMENSIONS

Science, which is a name for a path, way, or school: is now talking about multiple dimensions <Scientific American November 2003: Strings & Spacetime With 11 Dimensions>. But, in the science that surrounds the core string called The Bible, several different realms or dimensions have been revealed. One dimension is called Heaven, while another dimension is called Hell. As the biblical text states in the masters house there are many mansions. It could be thought of as being said that in the two major states of being in the next world, they will also be divided by levels; and hence we have Dontaes Inferno <St. Matthew 7:13> <which is harder: 1) to create an ark to save a select few from an Earth wide flood, or 2) to create an artificial black hole "DNA" type super shreder> <by the way, did anyone else other then them on the ark survive the flood <infrahuman, giant, H. georgicus, Homo habilis, H. erectus, H. rudolfensis, H. ergaster, H. sapiens, H. heidelbergensis, H. neanderthalensis <H. habilis, H. erectus, H. sapiens> <Scientific American November 2003 Stranger In A New Land Page 82>> ?>!

SEE THE EMF

How can you see what is called the Kundalini force without having the "mystical" experience? The human body contains in it electricity which you can see if you look at the point when you are shocked by touching metallic objects. This allows you to see the exchange of energy and electricity in specific from your body to and through the object. And this is what the raw Kundalini system can said to be about. The path or paths that the electromagnetic force can travels through your human system. Naturally, this system is regulated by what is called your rhythm, but it can be directed or tapped into by your breathing pattern and / or mental focus. Hence the introduction of the mind intention arts such as Chi Kung, Tai Chi, Kung Fu, Karate, Yoga, etc. But sometimes you can feel the electric motor force of the body without all of that. Just write long enough!

IN EGYPT

The Bible has many things to say about Egypt. Even Jesus was said to have gone to Egypt. If we cipher the name Egypt itself we could say: "e" equals the five <external> star of man himself, "g" equals the seven global, or sphere chakras hidden within or behind the flesh of man, the "y" is the letter "e" raised up beyond the "o" <the "e"> implying natural motion, the "o" being the "e" once activated an expanded like the fertilized egg, the "y" being a cup to hold the mystical fluid from the tail of the "y" that extends and coils below. The "y" also stands for the power of the yod <in Hebrew> which implies "the <hidden god> hand". The "p" being the sixth chakras activated. When the chakras become activated, the "knower" or person is said to be able to "see" <"c", "m" <three humps, mounds, pyramids>, "w" <the two cups of ida and pingala active within the three vertical ways> the <inner> light. This inner light signals the activation of the immutable seed into the completed second <immutable> body. And where does all of this happen? At the cross! How many crosses are there? Three in the body <moving> up right, and one on the side of the central cross <which implies the releasing of the activated seed from the <little box> into the mixing box <coffer> central chamber shaft <risen obelisk> <base of the spine> at the base of the neck into the bowl of the skull <called the mystical cup that holds the waters of life>. The solar seed is said to move up the Nile <of the spine> to the calm waters of the basin or cup <of the skull> in the mystical boat of Ra. Are there any boats in Egypt? Just imagine, if a boat is upon the Nile or in the dry dock, pit, or coffer container> when the Nile floods, who knows how high upward the boat might be raised? Then when the waters recede, where might the boat land? Up on a pyramid?

PI LIE

Pi times the radius squared equals what? If you can answer this question, you just might be the greatest genius this world has ever known. And if you can draw a circle using measurement and instrument with the constant pi you might just be the greatest drafter of this world has ever known. And if you can explain how you were able to draw that circle using pi, and show your completed circle; you might just be the father of a lie. And if you can build a house based upon the formula of pi, you might just be the son of a lie. And if you can teach others your grand concept, you might just be the professor of a lie. All I want you to do is define the meaning of Pi as a mathematical number. Three point one four is not pi, so don't even try. Here is a reflection of pi! Wide is the difference between 3.14 and 3.1415926535. I believe the answer is .0015926535. Not very much is it, unless you're talking about being accurate, correct, and exact. Suppose you had 31 billion, 415 million, 926 thousand, 535 dollars in the bank. Now you want to buy a spaceship to go to the moon. You withdraw all the money, which is exactly what you need. But the teller gives you, in check form, 31 billion, 400 thousand dollars and zero cents. Oh my, first of all your coming up short on your purchase; and second, where is the rest of the money? Or is it that you don't care? I have heard that some of you just don't care <but you might in The Day Of The Light>! Some things make me wonder about the students and the teachers. I stumbled upon this "level" of mathematical accuracy in high school. It involves three elements. The plus sign, the minus sign, and the zero. See, that which I just said is a truthful wrong. I began to use the "term value" for a number, and use zero as a placeholder <like a computer does with binary code>. I always used the positive or negative sign along with zeros before numbers involved in calculations. For example, one plus ten would be converted into positive zero one plus positive one zero. It became a form of science to me. And later on I found the same point been made about the square <or squared, I am not sure> root of negative five being really one times the square root of negative five. The number one as a power is implied. What I also found interesting is that certain numbers can be said to be bipolar or orientation perspective specific. In a strange way, this attitude towards a written figure explains the affect of the will upon “dark matter”. We might say that the number nor dark matter are magical, only that the way they are used due to the viewers mind results in a form of “mind intention”. And for those whom enjoy math and music, let the disc jockey play about the function of “x” as it approaches zero. By the way, I am sure you have noticed my “run on sentences”. Well do two things: first look at that 31 billion, second try to read a legal contract. My use of commas reflects what is called “the scientific method”. What is science? Am I a scientist? If I study two or more fields of study, what am I. Is science a multi polar term about one central core of understanding?

THE BOZO

<Ike Love : Movie: BELLY> But they got “The Boz Zo”! I liked the seventies. If you had a big bald spot in the center of your head, you could still be cool. You were proud of what ever you had. Yet, and as you walked down the street, fluffing the sides of your puff “fro”; you might sing: “oh no, I got the B. 0. Z. 0.; and if you can't spell it that's Bozo! I rake it to the left, and I picked it to the right; and they call me B O Z O, cause I played in hair all night though! Is Bozo really the worlds most famous clown, or is Bozo” an tribe in Africa <NFR> <they got the Bozo>!

FRONTER

<Poetic states of mind <notice states verses state>> can you lie? I heard a certain man explained the teaching of his mother catching him in the state of lying, he had become the lie. But when you try <“try”> to pass upon the lie, who do you fool? Oh, it is called to water down <about .01 proof> the truth. That is called weak. Look for the error called the lie. Can you see “The Truth”? If you can't see the lie, how can you think you can see the truth? You should lay <the body> in bed, not the lie! Ugly! Call it what you will. A lie.

Jesus did it! He called “out” the laws of men <lies against The Laws Of God The Father> by name. And notice, if he did not give the name, he asked <or questioned with authority>. Maybe he knew the name, but made the lie confess to the truth by “asking <demanding>” for its name. Not that he didn't know it was a lie, but also stating that how a group lies become to exist as one. A House of lies. Many lies connected together in union. Lie a linked to lie b, and so on. The lie by the assumption connection. It should be a law, that none can carry around in public a Bible unless: a) they are reading it <time period required>, or b) have read it. Just because you have one? Oh, how I “believe” in this <that which I have not read, so some say>? What kind of mental illness is that? “Know ye not the scriptures?” And that leads us to the powers <mathematical> of names. Each name was/is a mathematical formula. Adam is Adam, but <look at but the negative conjunction “but”> Adam is not Adam. Adam in Hebrew <upper level Kaballah> is a formula <see: The Powers Of Genesis>. Then you have the environmental affect that must be calculated. Did you read the book <The Bible>? Yes, first I read calculus <Psalms>, then I read parts of Mark <Metaphysics>. What a beautiful mind? Will a man rob God? Man will rob his own self <of ever lasting life, so says The Bible>! You stole from yourself. Just play in the hair all night long, but in the day <light>?

NIGHT RIGHT

What was the Night “made” for? 0h, so you could see the stars? Internal or external? Do you know why you are here? Where is the afterlife <which is a term that has a variable of “x” as time in it>? So the eternity does not have a variable of “x” as time <or time <motion>> related growth in it? Can you believe in ten dimensions, but not in a dimension called Heaven! It's the word sin. Snake <S in> inside of you <Kundalini>? If you could only understand that a dragon is not a dragon just because “you” <Adam> called it that!”! Oh, look at that Yogi. Who? Yogi. Oh, the bear. Yes, the Bear “that kills humans”! Don't be silly. But ease off if you have to for “these people” and so on!

DUMB

Naw, I am probably one of the dumbest people I have ever known. I recognized that, looking back, boy was that dumb! I read a lot. I became interested in a subject and become also shocked at how dumb I was about it. What feeling is there like saying you don't understand a subject in a room full of masters! Can you feel me? I understand the state of being called ignorant <to not know <know ye not>>, but is there a state called "beyond ignorance"? Is it? I now wonder, is that the state of being called a "fool"! It's one thing to play the fool, while its another <at the end of time> to be the fool! And where is the so-called fool's paradise? A squared plus B squared may equal C squared in an right triangle, but the square root of C <in general> has two possible answers!

SPIRITUAL VERSES MANIC

The term manic in the Western medical system is defined as being touched by the spiritual. But Western science, in general, does not define what aspect of the so-called spiritual an individual has been touched by <I hope to talk about this in something I call "House Of One Thousand Manics" <which deals with the unformatted mental structure>>. For example, a person can become involved with the study of rocks to the point that they start to associate the frequencies of the rocks to invoke emotional states. Once a "feeling" or radiation is acknowledged, this person has entered into a higher form of interface with the specific form of nature. They become what is called sensitive. Once their awareness of the rock power becomes part of their personality, either self perceived, or perceived by others, they become what is "called" the spiritual. This form of spirituality has to do with the feeling of radiant affect of the rock. By use of the perception facility called the will, they may be able to hear or differentiate the feeling of vibrations given off by certain rocks. This attention to the vibration goes beyond the average persons attention, thereby putting this person in another state, level, or classification. In general, they become part of a group that is called "spiritual". Now once the person starts to interact with the frequencies, willfully or not, they become classified as manic. They are said to have been touched by the spiritual. This means they are said to have reacted to a fine <or finer> vibration than average. One of the largest classifications in past times was the mood <mental> changes in some peoples behavior during certain phases of the moon. This particular science had to do with the affects and effects the motion of the spheres for zodiac. The zodiac signs were broken or divided into several types of events. The rise in of certain stars <as in the association with Sirius and the flooding of the Nile, the rising of Venus, etc.> and the motion of the moon, the motion of the earth about the sun, the appearance of comets, and so on. Data was compiled and compared mostly by birthdays, and so general hypothesis were made. In ancient times, the stronger one reacted within their statistical groping towards the general deviation, the more "spiritual" that individual was said to be. Also, the reaction rate and intensity was also a very important factor or indicator of the "spiritual" nature or sensitivity of that person. In a strange sense, this form of spiritual classification is similar to checking or watching for allergic reactions to certain chemicals. You also have people who are sensitive to certain electromagnetic motions; such as underground moving water. Then you have people who are said to be sensitive to certain vertical energies that extend from trees and upright stones <Stonehenge <an initiation temple of Keridwen, the Serpent Goddess <NFR MAP 251>>, obelisks, Sphinx>. Once the awareness to these energies become known, the attempting to feel these forces by those who could not, became certain types of schools. For example, in the so-called Asian art of Chi Kung, the students often "hug" trees to feel its radiant power. To the untrained, this practice looks and sounds hilarious. Now in the science Chi Kung, the body of man is considered to be as a walking bipolar tree. Each heel has an absorbing relationship with the energy the earth gives off, just as does the roots of the tree. And this statement in particular leads to another science called herbology. This herbology science dealt with the chemical and electromagnetic forces within certain plants. These were and are sciences that man originally used. Even animals were studied to see what plants they ate when they were sickly. Now I call the science of Chi Kung a so-called Asian art due to the facts I have discovered point towards Africa as their origin. In short, the Egyptians are said to have worshiped the sun.

Well, while some might have thought the sun was God, which is a form of idle worship; incorporated into the general religious practices was the acknowledgement of the positive effects of the solar power. Again this is directly related to the study of plants and animals. This studying of the energy of the sun evolved into basic postures or best ways to collect the energy. The postures were said to direct the solar power into specific parts of the human body. Once the relationship between different parts of the body became known, the postures became linked together to form a phasing circuit of input energy. As the knowledge of the energy order or Earth rhythm increased, so did the postures to "feel" and "feed" that organ or bodily system. Once two or more of the postures were linked together, they became what is called "a form" <or circuit>. Now "this form" was fine if done in only the same geographical area as its origin; but as people moved about the ball the earth, so did the solar and earth power output vary. The form had become specific to sun angles and magnetic polarity. So, although the basic teaching of the form would stay the same, it would change due to geographical location. And due to stronger or weaker energies, sometimes the posture would change to carry the varied input intensity. Hence, the change in the outward appearance of "the form". But one of the real secrets of this way, circuit, or form of energy induction is called "mind intention". This is where the student is able to tune in, channel, amplify lesser energies, or even change energies frequencies, and redirect them at will. Think of it like this: electricity can be made either chemically or magnetically, but it is still the electricity <electromotive force> that is desired. Again, once the student could "feel" the energy, which is part of the elementary stage, they were said to be coming spiritual. Why am I explaining all of this? Because I want to make clear that to be so-called spiritual or manic has generally to do with relating to finer vibrations of specific orders. Why have I not said anything about church, bible, etc.? Well, in the ancient science, when someone was sensitive to these things, called "The Godly Order", the person was said to be able to see behind the second door or veil <that which is hidden>. In Western terms, metaphysics was a higher form of physics. It can generally be stated that one might say physics can be affected by metaphysics. And if you were the one to say this, you might be laughed right out of town. It would be like entering into a coin toss bet for very high stakes and calling “neither”! Get it? Heads or tails? Neither! But you have a fifty percent chance if you choose according to statistics and quantitative analysis. That fool is going to lose! So the whole town comes out to mock and laugh at Meta <which is short for the use of metaphysics <well maybe, ah pause ya! editors note>>. All bets are in. The man <dummy> flips the coin in the air. The whole town grows wild entering into an metaphysical endorphin induced psychedelic transcendental drunken stupor. And the coin lands upon the floor. Guess what? The coin is standing upon the rim. See! Metaphysics! Now the question becomes, did Meta influence the coin in some way with his mind <intention>? Well, this question is now a valid form of reasoning once dark matter is considered. But it could also have been quantum calculations and swag <scientific wild ass guess>. How could it be due to swag? Because Meta knew of a variable that they were “totally” ignorant of. The odds were not fifty to fifty. Well, not fifty-fifty in specific! Did Meta break the laws of physics? No! Then what was it? Metas science was more refined than theirs. But how could Meta have known? Meta didn't. Then why did Meta choose “neither”? Because Meta could “feel” a tremble in “the force”! What force? The force above the standard general force of fifty to fifty <a moment or place of fluctuation <at an torii <looks like the sign for pi, which is called an transcendental number>>>. So what does this have to do with the Sun, spiritual, and manic? Well, the Egyptians tried to explain that there are greater and lesser forces in the natural order that extend from the “divine” order. The Egyptians tried to explain that they could “feel” and come to know that there was a higher order behind that of the Earths Sun <which might not be the brightest star <and if it is not, then it is a false light>>. Of course the Sun would represent the zodiacs <lesser and greater> and the mathematical orders. Strange motions, glitches, or abnormalities are what they are called. Variations in the motion of the sky that defy the mathematical laws in general: “As above, so below”. That was the general specific formula. It would be the same as saying <a statement and a question in one>: how can you get more out of a simple equation if you don't put more in! So therefore, if there is a sudden change and return <quantum motion, explainable by x and y, a multiple movement like having a chess royal piece upon a checker game, but the opponent doesn't know it> in a mathematically known <calculus, geometry, trigonometry>

system, then there must be an outside <or unknown> <to The Unknown God> influence. And this type of thought could be derived from the motion of the solar sphere upon the sundial. Hence, the proof through nature of the existence of "The One" that did and does cause variations <from and on> above. But that is only looking upward <as above>. So if you put a stick <fishing pole> into the Nile River and look into the water, you may notice the stick appears to bend. Then you say oh. As above, so below. Then the question becomes where is the bottom of the stick? Soon you learn to adjust for light refraction so you can spear fish. Then you say ah! And so the assumption that the divine plane is above and before the earth plane, but is hard to see due to the substance that separates them causes an bending appearance. And between the two, a type of water <the waves or bent lines> in which you need a special boat <solar disc <disco>, seed, flower, or ladder> to carry you <or your will <mind>> across. Hence the unseen world! The next natural thing to do is to statistically "watch" those whom say they have been in contact with "an" unseen world and compile data again. Some say this and that will happen, and it does. They are also called Prophets. Some don't know what was going to happen, but they seem to "feel" transitions. Calculations were made. Data was compiled. Take the record of Moses. Now it is said he made, or had contact with The Living God in a bush that did not burn in form. This would be considered his <Moses'> contact point, but it would be concluded that he was touched or was being guided much earlier than that in his life. As Moses told the story of the changes in his life that were not usual, it would be perceived that he was being led or induced towards a certain point. Now because of the intense nature of his contact with this "rate of change", he <Moses> would become one whom reveals <reveling, Revelation> his perception of the force that caused his change. If his knowledge, as it did, exceeds that which is generally known, he may have higher <called new> insights into this "divine force". As he <Moses> presents his factual data to the "religious" organization of his studied order, his new or revealed insights may differ from what is known to date. His new revelations will be met with resistance. Now who is in touch? He that is being led, or they that are in pursuit? He that is being led of course! So what might they say about him who is revealing higher or finer signs of the divine force. They call him a heretic. And hence, Akanoten and Moses as <are> one in the same <aka no ten, or aka not ten, one, net, t = 20, one t, tone, word, sound>. Well if not ten, then what? Aka a yod. And who is Akaayod? A reflection of The Aleph. How? The Yod is a folded or compressed Aleph. How? Place a aleph inside a zero, envelop, shell, blackhole, cosmic dot, or container and compress it.>! Heretic: one who holds religious opinions contrary to the doctrines of his church, or a dissenter from accepted beliefs or dogma of any kind. And in specific, they said the same about Jesus in his teaching about the "tradition" of washing hands before eating. And hence, they called him "mad" <a form of manic> with a demon. I wonder if they heard the part about "my only begotten son" and what they thought then. In addition, the fact that there are fish in the waters below would cause wonder about above. So if there is a place of life <water, deep, deaths, sea, ocean> below, there must be life above. Now the mathematicians won't say that, but they will say dimensions. So far they are on the tenth dimension. I just wonder if any of those they call Hell. Why should some choose Hell? Because they might say: "just because it exists, does that mean we should go there!"

Hidden Genesis Code
Jean Houston: The Powers of Genesis

THE POWERS OF GENESIS
by Jean Houston
[The following is the text of a mystery school talk.]

The Power of Projective Language

Let us begin by considering a people in the distant future who are entirely tone deaf and without music suddenly discovering musical notation. They could analyze it, interpret it as a variation on ordinary speech, but they could not hear it, and would have no comprehension of the concept of music. If one of their number then took enormous pains to rediscover music by determining that these notations are really signs for sounds of different tones, and then re-trained his brain and nervous system out of being tone deaf so that eventually he could actually hear different tones and then chords and then musical phrases, eventually he would be able to hear musical themes and then symphonies. He then understands the need for instruments to express these tones and reinvents musical instruments. He becomes a musician in a tone deaf world, a world that has no conception of what it cannot conceive, and no notion of instruments for music. What happens if he performs for an intelligent audience on these instruments. Most would shuffle their feet uncomfortably at this strange noise. Quite a few would walk out deeply offended by this esoteric claptrap. Others would try to analyze the variations in this speech pattern–thinking it an especially interesting version of glossolalia, while a very few would have stirrings of memory from the time that music could be heard. It is thought that "it has been kept alive in them because it happens that the interpretation of the musical notation as ordinary speech is so devised that the symphonic themes appear as a kind of echo under the guise of poetry" (Cipher of Genesis, p. 3). The exposure calls to a repressed but still available potential within them; they could still wake up to music and even the possibility of becoming musicians. Music, like mathematics, is a projective language. A good musicians reads a score and hears it: it is projected as energy transforms inside his being. The same is true of a fine mathematician who reads mathematical symbols and internally performs the pattern of mathematical operations of which the symbols are the projection. Now there are a few ancient languages that are also, at certain levels, projective languages. Discuss why this tends to be so only [for] ancient languages.

Among them are Sanskrit, high Javanese, and most fully realized–Old Hebrew. The sounds and portraits of their alphabetic characters perform multiple musics on several levels of understanding. in Sanskrit the fundamental syllables, called "bija" syllables like "Om", "Ram", "yam", are thought to be the primary codings of the energies of the Universe and of Creation...

With regard to Hebrew an ages-old traveling and hiding mystery school has been developed around the implicit content of the projective dimensions that are there to be received in Hebrew. The name of this mystery school is the Qabala. The word Qabala means: that which is received. And what Qabala says is that the twenty-two glyphs which are used as letters in the Hebrew alphabet are in fact and in essence twenty-two proper names originally used to designate different states or structures of the one cosmic energy, which is the essence of semblance of all that is. However, although these letters correspond to numbers, symbols and ideas, they exceed all classifications. The letters themselves, Aleph, Bayt, Ghimel, etc., are projections, codings of biolically structured energies in different states of organization. And it would seem that primary languages provided ontological linkages with the essence of the objects objects specified. We would ask, why is the left hemisphere of the neo-cortex-what we may refer to as the speech center or even the logos–laser so large? Because it is meant to be the transducing vehicle for the cosmic languages and codings.

What a modem Qabalistic scholar like Carlos Suares suggests is that there is extraordinary substance in the Biblical account of the archetypal myths and quasi-historical episodes recorded in Genesis which is not there to the surface eye. Most of us, even good scholars among us, read Genesis from a tone-deaf perspective, not with the eye and the ear that is attuned to Qabala to the receiving of the incredibly complex cosmic history which is codified within the projective resonance of the Hebrew letters.

Read with the musician's or Qabalistic ear, a Biblical account is not only the record of the wanderings of a Semitic tribe and their patriarchs, it is, he says, “a concealed record of the actual events of the projection of the Cosmic Drama into the biosphere” <P.26>. Suares also feels that “the names and the quasi-historical events recorded in the Bible are, regarded from the point of view that only 'ordinary' history occurs, fixed in time and space to definite individuals and periods. This is probably indeed the case, judging from the results of contemporary Biblical research.” <Discuss Biblical archeology and what we learn of Abraham's wanderings and Joseph in Egypt.> “But if there is also a sacred history, it escapes from time and space save for those tremendous historical moments, the kairoi, such as the time of Christ, when the two histories coalesce into one. The “time of Abraham” may have been also such a time, or it may not have been. It may be that the sacred history has become, for convenience, grafted onto the account of secular history given in the Bible.”

A Few Notes and Brief Excursion on the History of Qabala

Before I go any further, I'd like to offer a few words on what the Qabala is. Rabbi Philip Berg, the director of a kabbahstic institute and press in New York, and one of the world's leading Kabbalistic scholars, says, “Into this mysterious universe we are born, with no apparent set of instructions, no maps or equations, no signs or guideposts, nothing but our equally unfathomable instincts, intuitions, and reasoning abilities to tell us where we came from, why we are here, and what we are supposed to do. What we do possess–perhaps it is the key to our survival as a species–is an almost unquenchable need to know. A human being comes into this world with a passionate sense of wonder and inquisitiveness and an equally powerful need for self expression. yet, somehow these seemingly indelible primal imperatives become eroded, as a rule, after only a few years' exposure to modem reality and contemporary educational methods.” Berg strongly suggests that his way, the way of Qabalah with its symbols and tools, is a major key to finding the answers. In fact, in his book The Kabbalah Connection, he actually says, “The alef-bet is a cable representing the missing link between the sending of a message from the physical to the metaphysical level.” In 1983,

Berg who was then the much esteemed director of the Institute for Kabbalah in Jerusalem, delivered a paper entitled "Extra-Terrestrial Life in Outer Space: Forces Behind the Future." He spoke of Hebrew as very likely being a kind of cosmic computer code for programming our "walking bio-computers," and said that the great kabbalistic book, the Zohar, linked with certain Biblical chapters, especially Genesis, provided an excellent system for contacting extraterrestrial intelligence. In other words, in qabala are to be found the ways and means of reprogra our body-minds into higher vibratory forms that make of us a kind of metacomputer able to contact universal codes and intelligences. Indeed, there are esoteric kabbalists who believe that Genesis is a kind of code book written by some ultra-terrestrial intelligence for those spiritual hackers who can figure it out.

We will be operating in our exploration of the book of Genesis on the supposition that the historical character of the Bible is really twofold, just as the Hebrew language is twofold. The Hebrew language can be used as ordinary speech or it can be, as you will soon see, used as a projective experience. The historical aspect of Genesis conveys not only ordinary history <that there were wandering tribes coming out of Ur of the Chaldees some 4000 years ago–with all their sheep and cows and chattel> but, hidden within that, a sacred history concerned with the stages and working out on earth of this cosmic drama. This may be why the Hebraic text was preserved so very accurately over thousands of years.

Thus, the finding of the Dead Sea Scrolls and with it the text of Isaiah from the first century–which is virtually the same, letter for letter, as our previously earliest known text from a thousand years later.

The Nine Archetypal Letters

To begin to understand the qabalistic interpretation of the deeper meaning of Genesis and why it is not just a collection of folk tales, we have first to explore the interior meanings of the nine archetypal letters. The ancient texts are preserved so rigorously because every letter and the pronunciation of every word is taken as significant. The Qabala tells us what the Hebrew letters are made of and shows us how each letter is not simply an initial but is a word complex: an equation. When we say via", we mean "a"; in Hebrew you would say ALEPH. ALEPH is made up of ALEPH, LAMMED, PHAY, and LAMMED and PHAY are made up of many other living characters, each of which is filled with meaning as you can see and which branches and rebranches like a tree, a living organism or a most elaborate chemical compound. This is a form of hieroglyphic thought rendered in alphabetic characters in such a way that the Hebrew characters introduce us to a language capable of conveying depth of meaning and complexity virtually without limit, yet remaining within the limited bounds of our capacity for thought. When studied, it activates in us, as music did for the tone deaf with residual memory, an uncoding of tremendous knowledges which have been forgotten or perhaps which are so deeply coded in us that we have been unaware of their existence. In fact, I would go so far as to suggest that what it uncodes in us is our future possibility, the culture that we are painfully moving towards, the culture no longer just homo faber, the tool maker, but of homo mondo faber–the world maker.

As Suares says, "It is a code which uses these equations and not ordinary words as we are accustomed to use them. It trains the mind to hold together, all at once, a complex structure, each part of which is relevant to every other part." <Discuss why the Jews, as the holder of so many of the structures of existence, have been able to survive in spite of the entropy of antagonistic cultures that have tried to suppress them.> The reading of Genesis then becomes the reading and the experience of a living code of creation and transformation; the keys to the transforming of culture and society, and even of world making. This is obviously a subject which could take many, many lives of inquiry. Within one weekend, albeit within the subjective and eternal time of a mystery school, we can only dip into a fragment of a fragment, but let us just do that briefly now so as to set up a few musical cadenzas in your mind for your experience of the cosmic drama of creation which is implicit in the musical notation called Genesis. Take the first letter, ALEPH. In the depth understanding of the Qabala, the symbol ALEPH is used to project a concept of an unthinkably immense energy, hyperspatial and hypertemporal, transcending time and space, without which nothing could exist, operating within the structure of everything as that by which it is able to be. ALEPH projects into us a constant awareness of the mystery of existence. Although it is not thinkable, we participate in it on many levels that it thinks its way through us. Perhaps it is correspondent to the Chinese Tao. Alone among an Hebrew letters, ALEPH has no pronunciation of its own and according to where it is placed in a configuration of letters it can be sounded as any of the vowels, so ALEPH transcends all logical use in language just as a concept it transcends all understanding. For the Qabala to be sacred means to partake of this mystery of ALEPH Everything that exists is sacred because it is inhabited by ALEPH. <Discuss the ALEPH point and read from the Borges story about the ALEPH in the Possible Human.. Relate Aleph to Bohm's notion of the Implicate and the Superimplicate orders.> The first archetype letter is ALEPH, naturally. The second is BAYT. BAYT means house or physical support or container, any kind of dwelling. It is the complement of, and polarity, if you will, of ALEPH. It is the container, whereas Aleph is the immeasurable energy. BAYT may be seen as that which allows for the implicate to become explicate in time and space.

The third principle is GHIMEL.

GHIMEL has the meaning of change and transformation of energy. If there is ALEPH and BAYT together, there must occur a transformation of energy, for how is ALEPH going to flood into BAYT and how is BAYT going to contain any ALEPH at all without some fundamental change going on. GBIMEL gives us some clues to this mystery.

GHIMEL which is also related to camel, which stores and converts water, is the mystery of conversion of the energies of the life force.

The fourth projected archetype is the letter DALLET.

DALLET means resistance to disruptive forces. It is the principle of homeostasis and of restoration of that which is being disturbed. In atomic nuclei it is the role of the binding energy. It is the archetypal principle of challenge and response. If you have the flowing of energy in ALEPH, the attempted containment of this energy in BAYT, the conversion of this energy in GHIMEL, than you are certainly going to need the energy of DALLET to respond to all these challenges and bind it all together.

The fifth principle is the letter HAY.

HAY is the principle of life in itself and the tasks which life performs–that is transmitting impulses, maintaining balance, knowing the appropriate timing to release more life and conserve life, to adjunct to the requirements of the external and internal environment. It is the principle, ultimately, of keeping the ecology of energies going. If you are going to have the overwhelmingness of ALEPH flooding into the containment of BAYT with the help of the conversion of these energies by GHIMEL and the binding of all of these energies together in DALLET, then you have to have the sensitivity of the life of HAY to keep all of these principles functioning equitably and ecologically.

The sixth principle is VAV.

VAV is the archetype of fertility projected into living organisms as the function of reproduction.
It is the power of perpetuation connecting the old with the new and assuring existence in time. If you have the cosmic energies of ALEPH into the containment of BAYT being changed and converted into the energies of GHIMEL, bound together by DALLET, and equalized by the life Expression of HAY, then, if you want all of this to continue, you've got to have the reproductive function of VAV.

The seventh principle is the letter ZAYN.

This means archetypally structured movement towards indeterminate potentialities. It is motion towards an entelechy that is calling. If you have the immensities of ALEPH attempting to indwell in BAYT, undergoing the energy conversion of GBEVEL, held together by DALLET, within the life form of HAY, and reproduced in VAV, then it has to be called forward to its next unfolding in a motion of ZAYN.

The eighth archetypal principle is the letter HHAYT.

This is the concept of the storehouse of potentialities, the pool of patterns and genes, if you will, that are there to be accessed and which can be used to give form and creative innovation to structures in this world. If you have the cosmic energies of ALEPH contained in the house of BAYT converted to the energies of life of GHIMEL held together by the binding energy of DALLET within the life form of HAY, reproduced by VAV, set into motion towards indeterminate potentialities by ZAYN, then all of this is going to find the new patterns for the next stages of the coding in HHAYT.

The ninth archetypal principle is the letter TAYT.

TAYT is the womb place of gestation, of bringing all these archetypal energies into new genesis for the new creation in time of the cosmic drama that was begun by ALEPH–the immensity of cosmic energy, projected into the container of BAYT, transformed into the living energies of GHIMEL, held together by the binding forces of DALLET, within the ecological life principle of HAY, reproduced by VAV, and set into motion towards new learning by ZAYN, found in the storehouse of potentials of HRAY, and all of these together re-gestated in the place of new genesis to TAYT. This is the multidimensional thinking implicit in the sacred reading of Hebrew as found in Genesis.

According to Qabala, when ALEPH is projected into existence-in-time, it becomes YOD. YOD symbolizes the assertion of existence. The Hebrew symbol is a hand. By this it becomes limited and within the framework of time sequences. It also is coded in the notion of the hand of God reaching out to start existence as in Michelangelo's painting on the ceiling of the Sistine chapel. This implies a sacrifice on the part of AILEPH of its own unique character. It compromises its nature when it becomes YOD and is thereby involved in contradiction. The war with time enters all existence and becomes a conflict between time and eternity, ALEPH and YOD. This is the great Cosmic Game, the Cosmic Drama– the tension between ALEPH and YOD. If we search for the outcome of this cosmic game and why it is at all, we are asking for the meaning of QOF, which is the symbol for 100, and higher reconciliation. ALEPH <1> finds its limited time existence in YOD <10> and its fulfillment in QOF <100>. In QOF the division is reconciled. Number symbolism is critical in Qabalistic thought. For example, the symbolic age of 100 reached by Abraham when his son Isaac was to be born <previously his name, Abram, had been changed by the addition of HAY, meaning lease of new life. Previously Abram-whose original name means top Daddy or

exalted Pop, is changed by God by an addition of HAY, meaning lease of new life <father of multitudes, exceedingly fruitful>. His wife, Sarai, has her name, originally meaning Queenie, similarly enhanced by the addition of the HAY and her name, Sarah, means mother of all nations. <By the way, the original name in Egyptian, Abram means "he who is father of the sun", or "he who possesses the sun". In Tibetan, Ram means the basis of the world. In Sanskrit, Ram is God, as in Rama. In the Celtic languages, Ram equates to universal essence. In Qabala, Ram means cosmic dwelling.>

There is also a further coincidence that may have immense cross cultural significance; it is this: ABRAHAM with the order of letters very slightly changed, looks like BRAHMA, scripture of India dating actually from around the time of Abraham. The coincidence signifies, according to the Qabala, that the traditional revelations of Abraham and Brahma are essentially one and the same in source. The fact that the Aleph is the first letter of the one, the last of the other, points to a single revelation which is split in two. Could it be that at some actual moment of history, ordinary and sacred history merged and a new dispensation spread over the earth both east and west?"

Website: http://www.psyche.com/psyche/txt/powers_of_genesis.html.

ETERNAL EGYPT CIPHER PART TWO

<Page 91> Round top Stela: excerpt: Earlier examples of relief in this catalogue demonstrate ways in which the interaction of hieroglyphs and images helped to determine the look of Egyptian two-dimensional art, both in the details of individual representation <cat. No. 6> and in the composition of whole scenes <cat. No. 2>. This Middle Kingdom stela exemplifies the Egyptians' strong preference for balanced, symmetrical designs. But the balance is weighted in an unusual way. A father and son stand facing each other. Their figurers follow the standard two-dimensional conventions of profile head and frontal eye, frontal shoulders and torso in profile but with the navel visible, profile buttocks and legs, with identical single-toed feet. The two are identical in almost every other respect as well: they are the same size; they both have the short, curly hairstyles that were especially popular during the early Middle Kingdom; and their kilts, with stiffened front panels and decorated belts, and their beaded necklaces and bracelets are almost identical. Each man holds a long staff and sekhem scepter, standard symbols of authority <cf. Cat. No.8>. On the figure facing right, it is clear that the staff is held in the left hand and the scepter in the right. The figure facing left, in the secondary position, is represented as a mirror image of the first. But since he, too, must be understood to grasp the staff with his left hand and the scepter with his right, the hands have been reversed <cf. Cat. No. 6 and 14>. The need to convey correct information superseded any visually jarring effect. The long column of text down the center tells us that the stela was dedicated to his father by the count <an honorific title> and overseer of priests Sensobek, 'his beloved son, his favorite, who causes the name of his father to live while he <the farther> is still on earth.' Such inscription appear on many stelae and statues of men or couples, and often the son is also represent, sometimes with other family members as well. But the lesser importance of his figure, and theirs, is almost invariably made clear in one or more ways-leftward orientation, smaller size, reverent pose-and of course, in the inscriptions. Here, however, the dominant figure, who faces right like the hieroglyphs, is the son. His name and titles are given a second time in the rightward-facing

line just above his head. The father, Intef, also a count and overseer of priests, is identified only once, in the leftward-oriented signs above his head. Even the column of text that invades his space belongs to Sensobek; it names his mother, Bebi. Presumably she was Intefs wife, but that is not stated here. The secondary position of Intef on his stela cannot possibly have been meant to imply disrespect; in ancient Egypt, such treatment of a parent would have been unthinkable. Rather, the unusual composition suggests that this stela was designed for a family offering chapel, where it would have been positioned along the left side, so that Intef faced outward. In this position it would have been auxiliary to one or more stelae dominated by <rightward-oriented> images of Intef himself. During the Middle Kingdom, many families built the little mudbrick chapels at Abydos, along the processional route of the god Osiris. These chapels housed statutes <see cat. No. 25> and stelae. It is likely that this stela was made for such a chapel at Abydos, where the spirits of Intef and Sensobek could, as they say in the brief prayer to Osiris at the top, 'see the beauty of the Great God, Lord of Abydos.'" <note: dos>. First I would like to comment upon a cipher of the word Abydos. Ab or aba <the "a" can be implied by the "y", yod, or hand> which means father of. The "y" again can be considered as "y" for yod or being the number five times two <beth> implies the five points of man raised to the third <"e", "o", or "uy"> power. The three powered force in the human body being the kundalion system <Ida, Pangala, and Sushumna <hint: reaching sahasrara>> which are fully activated by the yod, hand, or will of the father self to raise the his own son <sun, solar seed, immutable <body> self. While one is called the father, and the other son <sun, Ra>, they are connected by a sort of mirror image of each other. Remember that once Jesus resurrected into the second body, some did recognize him. But some did not recognize him <but he knew himself>. Think of a situation where the butterfly could see his own caterpillars <cat-a-ha pillar <obelisk>>>. Now that is to different forms from the same creature. Truly a bipolar creature. But the Phoenix lore is about the rebirth of the self. In addition, the "stiffened kilts" indicate the active phallus power. Sometimes there is a scene of a crouched man with an ankh <key of life> extending from his phallus area. This is also an indication of the active or charged phallus power, but does not necessarily mean that the kundalini system is awakened or has fired. But this stela also says that the sun and the moon <which is lit by the sun> are active. By the way, if the sun is out, we call that day, if the moon is lit or dark we call that night; but what do we call it if the sun and moon are out <or visible> at the same time as the sun?

<Page 92> Sesostris 1 <excerpt> “Sesostris I: From Karnak Middle Kingdom, Twelfth Dynasty, reign of Sesostris I [ca. 1965-1920B.c.] Granodiorite <see The Diamond Man> with large feldspar inclusions Height 31 in. [78.5 cm] EA 44, acquired in 1838, gift of R. W. H. Vyse. This forceful image depicts Sesostris 1, second king of the Twelfth Dynasty, striding bare chested and wearing a royal headcloth and a kilt with narrow pleats. Enclosed in a cartouche and carved in large hieroglyphs, the king's prenomen, Kheperkare, decorates the center of the wide belt holding his kilt in place. The attitude is traditional, but few of Sesostris I's many preserved statues depict him striding. He is more commonly shown in the form of a sphinx, kneeling, seated on a throne [alone or as part of a group], or in Osiride form. This is the only preserved statue that depicts him both striding and wearing a royal nemes headcloth. The thick body of the royal uraeus cobra, its hood now broken away, completes five turns as it winds over the top of the king's pleated headcloth. The wide back pillar covers the back of the headcloth and narrows at the top in the form of an obelisk. In the Middle Kingdom, back pillars do not otherwise extend over the headcloth - here it is an archaizing element recalling Old Kingdom royal sculpture. Presumably, Sesostris I commissioned this statue for the temple he erected for the god Amun-Re at Karnak, where it was found by a British officer, Richard W. H. Vyse, during his 1835-1837 excavations there. 'This statue does not fit readily into the stylistic framework associated with sculptures of the king at Karnak. The attitudes and the materials of Sesostris I's statuary vary greatly. His long life and reign, his active presence throughout Egypt, and the variety of stones used for his sculptures - each requiring a different approach to the material - are all factors contributing to the remarkable number and variety of his representations. Sesostris I's images include many stylistic variations that evolved during his forty-five

years in power. They range from the vigorously pompous colossi found at Tanis to finely modeled and delicately detailed statues with naturalistic features, excavated at Lisht. <paragraph 4> Distinct from both of these, statues carved in the style generally associated with Kanak are characterized by cheerful, stylized features, with large eyes and mouths that are almost hieroglyphic in form. While some features are similar on this statue - the rectangular face, the square set of the masculine chin, and the thick stylized ears set of high on the head - other features conteast notaably with most Sesostis I Karnak sculptures. For example, the dignified expression and the comparatively small, plastically modeled eyes are unique on images of the king associated with Karnak. The possibility that this statue was made elsewhere and then brought to Karnak cannot be excluded, but no good parallels have been found elsewhere, which suggests that this is another of Sesostris I's stylistic variations. Due to damage, the form of the mouth can only be conjectured. A naturalistic mouth would complete the image aesthetically. However, the extremely wide rounded corners preserved at the sides of the mouth and the full shape of the lower lip suggest that the king's mouth was highly stylized with almost evertrd lips, significantly altering the apparent naturalism of his expression." Yes, it is true that the same person could have two different looks <or representations> upon the same face; but what might the meaning be? Well, if the student or initiate was taught different phases of the same <kundalini> system at different temples, he will have different features on his statues showing his different halls of training. This is especially true if in this case his mouth has the extended smile to indicate the so-called "mystic trance" state of the firing of the kundalini system where it is said that the mouth locks close and so do the eyes. Yes, but his eyes are open. Well, let me say this, it is said that if you stare upon a candle or light bulb for a while, then suddenly turn off the light, then quickly close your eyelids, but look, you can "see lights inside your head". So if you can see lights moving inside your head, are your eyes open or closed? Hence, do you "see" the light verses if thy "internal" eye be one <implied: if your thinking be as The One, the one whose thought brought creation into existence>! And the back of his headdress express's the mystic rays extending from the firing of the pineal system.

<Page 93> The Nomarch's Retinue: Again the elements of this work are showing the acts of raising the immutable body. By the way, what is called the aura <ore <paddle, you dig - for ore> of Ra> is the light that seeps out of the body, just as "X" radiation <X-rays> seep into the body.

<Page 95> The Nomarch's Sister: It may or may not be a woman. The features of the <extended> breast and foot could imply the completion or advancement of the immutable <spiritual> body. The head ribbon implies the threefold power being advanced into the brain area. And also notice the flower <over the advanced> foot with three leaves. Look at the bands of power upon the hands and feet with three blue sections divided by white. The white meaning etheric as in what is called a spirit.

<Page 96> Block Statute and Niche Stela: <excerpt> "Block Statue and Niche Stela of Sahathor: From Abydos Middle Kingdom, Twelfth Dynasty, reign of Amenemhat II [qa. 1922-1878 B.C.] Limestone, traces of paint. A man named Sahathor is represented sitting on the ground with his crossed arms resting on his drawn-up knees. His body is covered by a cloak, from which only his open hands and bare feet emerge. Although the shape of the body is suggested, the form is so cubic that this type of statue is known in English as a block statue. To the ancient Egyptians, crossed arms in the presence of a superior signified respect and obedience. Since sitting on a chair was a sign of prestige, sitting on the ground was a humble pose. It was also a pose that could be sustained indefinitely - even today, in rural Egypt, caftanclad village men often adopt this pose to wait or to while away the time. Block statues were a Middle Kingdom invention. They first appeared early in the Twelfth Dynasty, at the same time that nonroyal persons started to place statues of themselves in temples, while continuing to provide their tombs with funerary statues. Middle Kingdom block statues have been found in temples and also in tombs. But they were not simply a new form of temple statue. As the submissiveness of the pose indicates, the block statue was intended to connect its owner with the cult of a god or the funerary cult of a king, to ensure protection in the Afterlife and also a magical share in the offerings provided for the cult each day. In tombs, Middle Kingdom block

statues were placed in a special chapel or even in a room outside the tomb proper. But since this was obviously a less efficient location for connecting to the cult than the temple, so most block statues were dedicated in temples, especially later, in the. New Kingdom [cat. nos. 45-47] and the Third Intermediate Period [cat. no. 121]. Sahathor's monument is something of a hybrid. The stela in whose niche it was placed was designed as a combination of a shrine and a false door. Architectural allusions include the cornice at the top and the figures of Sahathor, facing outward, in the thickness of the 'door' [cf. cat. no. 6a-b]. Only here, in this protected area, was any of the original paint preserved. Along with the standard offering prayer at the top, the inscriptions contain texts of a type found on tomb walls. False door elements include the offering scene at the top [cf. cat. no. 6c], which is shared by Sahathor's wife, Meryisis, the arrangement of his inward facing figures below the columns of text above, and the statue itself, since the owner's figure is sometimes shown facing outward from the central “doorway.” A false door often had an offering table placed directly in front of it, and so did this. Although all these details, architecture, and false door are appropriate to the tomb, this monument was not made for a tomb, but rather for a memorial chapel [cf cat. no. 20], one of many erected during the Middle Kingdom along the processional route at Abydos, which was the main cult center of Osiris and, it was thought, the site of his tomb. With its prayers to Osiris and another Abydos god, Anubis, and its vantage point along the processional way of The Great God, Sahathor's block statue combined the most potent aspects of tomb and temple representations of the deceased. “To me, this is a transition piece of artwork in a closed or hidden system. Sometimes the codes or ways of expression are changed. It is what is called a style in the thought of architecture. But sometimes it can express an advancement in knowledge. And while the statute may extend out of the doorway, the base of the door seems to fit. This whole work probably implies “the way of the hidden master”. This is a reference to one whom knows the secret of The Great Pyramid. Where it is its door? You could probably find the door it easier from the inside out than it was found from the outside in. And while the door is closed, would not the statue be in the “death” position <minus 90 degrees>? And now the statute is about to stand, exiting from darkness <the self inside the flesh shell> into the light <the light body self>. And in particular, this seated position is one of a few that is said to agitate the kundalini at the base of the spine. From the perspective of kundalini science, this statue shows the man sitting or balanced upon the three poles of the body.

<Page 98 - 103> “Feeling of not commenting due to repetition.”

<Page 104> Bust of the Seated Statue of Sesostris III: “Bust of a Seated Statue of Sesostris III: Provenance unknown: Middle Kingdom, Twelfth Dynasty, reign of Sesostris III [ca. 1874-1855 B.C.] Graywacke. More than one hundred statues and statue fragments of Sesostris III are known. They range in size from statuettes to colossi [see fig. 22]. Only a few of the smallest have survived more or less intact; the rest are incomplete or just fragments. This figure, the upper half of a seated statue, has lost, along with its lower half, the name of its royal subject. But the face is unmistakably that of Sesostris III. This is a rounder, less heavily modeled version of the face on the standing statue of Sesostris III [cat. no. 29]. Here, the expression, though sober, seems more bland. That is probably due in part to the virtual destruction of the mouth, which often carries much of the expression on smaller representations of Sesostris. The upper eyelids on the bust seem fleshier than on the standing figure. The upper lids droop over the lower lids at the outer corners, a standard mark of age on Egyptian sculpture from as early as the Second Dynasty, but one rarely found on representations of Sesostris. The ears, like the ears on almost all later Twelfth Dynasty sculpture, royal or private, are huge. <page 105 paragraph 3> Like the standing Sesostris III, this figure wears a nemes, a uraeus and an amulet suspended from a beaded cord. This amulet, found on royal statues from the middle of the Twelfth Dynasty on, appears on the majority of Sesostris III statues, rarely on representations Amenemhat III, and at least once at the very end of the Twelfth Dynasty. Since Egyptian kings were rarely shown wearing jewelry, other than the standard collar necklace and bracelets, occasionally paired with armlets and/or anklets,” this amulet is intriguing. To some, it looks like a little double pouch, pierced by a thorn. To others it resembles certain

amulets of the late Old Kingdom, some of which are equally enigmatic." Not really! The two spheres represent the sun and the moon, so to speak <if thy eyes be as one>. They also represent the crossing source of ida and pangala. The "bearded cord" represents the chakra power centers leading up to the rear base of the neck. Notice "the standard collar necklace" is missing, but the engraved lines appear the same as those about the head.

<Page 105- 107> "Feeling of not etc."

<Page 108> Kneeling Girl Holding Kohl Pot: <excerpt> "Kneeling Girl Holding Kohl Pot: From Thebes Middle Kingdom, Twelfth Dynasty [ca. 1985-1795 B.C.] This little figure kneels holding a vessel on a stand. Though large in relation to her, the pot is small and of the shape used in the Middle Kingdom to hold kohl ; [eye paint]. Though it came from a tomb, this object was first used during the owner's life: the top is scratched by the constant removal and replacement of the lid, which is now lost. The figure is clearly a young girl, with a high, pointed bosom, a thick pigtail growing from an otherwise shaven head and a calf-length skirt, over which she wears a hip belt of cowrie shells. An amulet in the form of a fish dangles from the curled end of her braid. Almost a dozen Middle Kingdom eye-paint containers of this type are known,' and all are very similar. In a few cases, the kneeling servant is so summarily carved that its gender is uncertain. Among those whose sex can be determined, one or two are definitely male, but most appear to be young girls, wearing a pigtail and a skirt. The girl's hairdo and jewelry are all typically Middle Kingdom. They were worn by young servants, which she probably is, but also by daughters of good families, because they had a protective, amuletic value. The pigtail, a variation of the sidelock worn by both male and female children since the Old Kingdom [cf. cat. no. 7], could itself be represented as an amulet because of its association with child gods. The fish, a symbol of regeneration, was also associated with Hathor. Worn by children, it may have been thought to protect against drowning. There are several examples of fish amulets with loops at the noses to suspend them in the same manner as the one hanging from this girl's braid. In a tale of the Middle Kingdom, a royal serving maid is described as

wearing [and losing] the fish pendant from her hair. On the wall of a Middle Kingdom tomb, the daughter of the tomb-owner is shown wearing one during an outing in the papyrus marshes. Cowrie shells were thought to resemble female genitalia, and so strings of cowrie shells or gold or silver cowrie amulets were often worn as hip belts by young girls to protect their fertility. Examples of sidelock, fish, and cowrie-shell amulets are all found on catalogue number 36. There could hardly be a greater contrast than that between this type of rigidly frontal Middle Kingdom figure, with its formulaic pose, and the lively, varied, usually asymmetric poses of the New Kingdom figures carrying cosmetic containers-not to mention the fact that the New Kingdom figures, when female, wear only jewelry [cf. cat. no. 81]. The use of such objects had not changed, nor had the underlying symbolism of regeneration and rebirth that caused them to be placed in the tomb. The differences between objects such as this one and catalogue number 81, for example, are primarily the product of huge changes in social customs and values during the three or four centuries that separated them." Well, every so often an author goes way out upon and limb! Like now! No it is not! While the statue may appear to be feminine, it may not be female. Anyway, where did the fish come from? Out of the bowl containing the water of life. So the fish or mystical seed travels up the two braided <ida and pangala> paths to the new cup <the skull>, but where will the water come from? The seated one drinking the mystical waters of life!

<Page 109> Pictorial Plaque: The same story except the staff of life has changed to show the three elements. Think of the staff as a combination of an inverted enlonged ankh and shepherds hook <crook <dumb ass 600 MgHz computer; work baby work; get off <on> the stage of Apollo <your life code unfolded <to the gates, yo!> <on life: file> <lock yo computer up and take controll: f<x> it <sets inside of sets> <ride on these!> <hay Wordell, day done gone cold 'manic' <coooomanic>>>, to stela fire <pi of ra> form to gods <guards>>. The lower part implies the kundalini base or seat. The middle part implies the spinal column. The upper part implies the turn at the medulla oblongata, the pineal position, the pituitary position, and the opening of the mystical door or hood of Ra!

<Page 110 - 114> “Feeling —— etc.”

<Page 115 - 116> Ptahemsaf: <excerpt>: “Ptahemsaf: Provenance unknown: Middle Kingdom, Thirteenth Dynasty [ca. 1795-1650 B.C.] Quartzite: The statue of Ptahemsaf, who was also called Senebtyfy, is carved in quartzite, a hard reddish stone that was especially favored in certain periods, including the later Middle Kigdom and the reign of Amenhotep III [cf. cat. no. 52]. Ptahemsaf stands with his left foot advanced and his arms at his sides. His head is slightly raised, an unusual feature, but one found occasionally on Egyptian sculpture of all periods- ‘In this case, Ptahernsaf's upward gaze may be related to the fact that his hands are not fisted, but held open in reverence; the image is one of worshiping the god in whose temple this statue was placed. For some time after the end of the Twelfth Dynasty, nonroyal people continued to be represented with faces based on the portraits of Sesostris III and Arnenemhat III, including their somber expressions. With few exceptions, 'these' late Middle Kingdom private portraits, 'as they are often called, are so clearly imitative that they cannot be considered portraits.' Nonroyal imitation of royal features was endemic to Egyptian art. However, this appears to be the only time in Egypt's long history when the royal models were past, not present, kings. Ptahemsaf's expression may seem more quizzical than serious, but his face is still a very much simplified version of Amenemhat III, with oval, heavy-lidded eyes, broad cheeks, and a full, rather prominent chin [cf. fig. 7]. Almost certainly this statue was made several generations after Amenemhat's death and was based, not on the actual royal portraits, but on subsequent representations of private people derived from them [male versions of cat. no. 40]. The long kilt is another of the enveloping garments favored by the men of the Middle Kingdom [cf. cat. nos. 25 and 28]. Wrapped around Ptahemsaf's body with its corners tucked in at the top, it covers him from breast to calf. This type of kilt, introduced during the later Twelfth Dynasty, became increasingly voluminous until, on examples such as this one, it balloons in front in a manner difficult to explain - assuming it really looked like this - except by the use of substantial padding. Garments like these were stored folded, in chests from which, being lined, they emerged well creased. The

sculptor has meticulously depicted these folds, showing the sharp inner creases as a single line and the softer outside folds - with a double line. The same 'realistic' touch had already appeared on a different type of long kilt worn by men of the later Old Kingdom and early Middle Kingdom. On at least one of the earlier examples, a wooden statuette, the folds and creases were lightly modeled in gesso." I don't think so! Out upon a limb again! You are seeing a transition in style. Something is under "the kilt". What? < Well go to page 120 the "Seated Senenmut." Now go to page 121. The "Block Statue of Inebny". Now go back to page 97. The "Block Statute and Niche Stela". Now go to page 91. The "Round-topped Stela of Intef and Sensobek". Now go to page 180. The "Kneeling Girl Holding Kohl Pot". Now go to page 84. The "Offering Bearer from Tomb Doorway". Now go to page 82. The "Stela of Tjetji". <Excerpt> Stela of Tjetji: From Thebes, tomb of Tjetji: "First Intermediate Period, pre-reunification Eleventh Dynasty [ca. 2112-2055 B.C.] Limestone: The stela of Tjetji reflects traditions of the late Old Kingdom and anticipates the best of the Eleventh Dynasty. It is divided into three unequal fields. At the top is a fourteen-line autobiographical inscription reading from right to left. The lower left portion depicts Tjetji facing right, in high raised relief, with two members of his staff; a small figure presents offerings before him. The lower right field is an elaborate offering prayer written in five vertical rows, listing wishes for the Afterlife. Tjetji's autobiography revives an Old Kingdom literary tradition nearly two hundred years after its disappearance. In Tjetji's era, autobioaphies typically praise nomarchs' efforts on behalf of their nomes. But Tjetji, a court official, returns to the Old Kingdom ideal of service to the king as the theme of his autobiography. He makes constant reference to his success in carrying out the king's wishes. This ideal continued to dominate subsequent autobiographies written during the Middle Kingdom. Tjetji recounts his service as overseer of the seal bearers of the king to Wahankh Inyotef II [2102-2063 B.C.] and Nakhtnebtepnefer Inyotef III [2063-2055 B.C.], establishing for historians the order of these kings. He also describes the borders of the Theban kingdom just before the reunification of Egypt under Nebhepetre Mentuhotep II [2055-200413.C.]. These borders stretch from Elephantine, in the south, to Abydos, in the north. Unlike later, extended autobiographies carved on tomb wall, this text is limited in length by the size of the stela. Yet Tjetji's use of the Egyptian language is striking and eloquent. Ronald J. Leprohon has recently suggested that this elaborate language, structured in tight grammatical patterns, derives from the deceased's own efforts to attain the ancient Egyptian ideal of 'Perfect speech.' Many commentators have noted the unusual shapes of some common hieroglyphs in this inscription.' For example, the mes sign in line 1, used to write the word “to give birth, to create,” could be read as an elaborate ankh sign used to write the word 'to live.' The scribe has created a visual pun that the ancient reader would surely have noticed. The relief, like the text above it, relates to the end of the Old Kingdom and anticipates the mature Theban style of the Eleventh Dynasty. The large figure of Tjetji and the subsidiary figures of his seal bearer, Magegi, and his follower, Tjeru, exhibit the features of this style. Cyril Aldred has identified the sharp ridge defining the edge of the lips, the accentuation of the muscles at the base of the nose, and the long earlobes as typical of both late Sixth Dynasty and mature Eleventh Dynasty relief styles. Edna R. Russmann has identified these same characteristics as elements of the Old Kingdom 'second style,' ancestor of the Theban style that's recognizable here. The Theban style also included high raised relief, deep sunk relief, and incised details. Gay Robins has pointed out the typically narrow shoulders, high small of the back and lack of musculature in the male figures. The details of Tjetji's face are also typical of the Theban style. The eye is large, outlined by a flat band representing eye-paint, and extended to form a cosmetic line that widens at its outer end. The inner canthus of the eye dips sharply downward. The eyebrow appears flat, rather than following the curve of the eye. The nose is broad, while the lips are thick and protruding. The lines of the lips end at a vertical line representing the cheek, rather than meeting in a point. The high quality of the relief 's execution demonstrates that the arts flourished in Thebes before the political reunification of Egypt. The layout and contents of the offerings spread before Tjetji are also typical of this period. The vertical columns of the offering prayer and Afterlife wishes, written from right to left, lead the eye toward the main figure. Previously the offering prayer was included in the introduction to the autobiography. Tjetji's stela illustrates the change position of the prayer, which will continue into the Middle Kingdom. Tjetji's stela clearly demonstrates that high standards of language and relief carving had been established in Thebes before political unification with Lower Egypt. These standards and their connection to the previous period of political unity perhaps point toward the early Eleventh Dynasty's conscious political plans for reunifying the country." But what type of kilt is that? Go to page 91. The "round-topped Stela of Intef and Sensobek". <Excerpt:> "and their kilts, with stiffened front panels." Stiffened is a polite way to express active sexual power." But what does the "kilt" look like? Go to page 17? Draw a vertical line down from the peak of the pyramid to <your> right of the Sphinx. What is that dark square? And what is the open square down and to <your> the right? Go To page 97. The "Block Statue and Niche Stela of Sahathor". But how does a person get into this position? First of all, the statue is sitting on three points <two feet and one point of the spine>. Now if his head is considered the cup or bowl, we could have a symbolic" Oracle of Adelphi

<<add el to phi> "Notice the word phi> < "When science meets religion at this ancient Greek site, the two turn out to be on better terms than scholars had originally thought. 'Questioning the Delphic <delta of alpha, beta, theta, and delta states of mind; and phi see> Oracle': Delphic Oracle is shown inhaling vapors in this photographic interpretation, because new evidence supports ancient assertions that intoxicating gases were a source of her inspiration. In reality, the gases would have been invisible. The temple of Apollo, cradled in the spectacular mountainscape at Delphi, was the most important religious site of the ancient Greek world, for it housed the powerful oracle. Generals sought the oracle's advice on strategy. Colonists asked for guidance before they set sail for Italy, Spain and Africa. Private citizens inquired about health problems and investments. The oracle's advice figures prominently in the myths. When Orestes asked whether he should seek vengeance on his mother for murdering his father, the oracle encouraged him. Oedipus, warned by the oracle that he would murder his father and marry his mother, strove, with famous lack of success, to avoid his fate. The oracle of Delphi functioned in a specific place, the adyton, or "no entry" area of the temple's core,

and through a specific person, the Pythia, who was chosen to speak, as a possessed medium, for Apollo, the god of prophecy. Extraordinarily for misogynist Greece, the Pythia was a woman. And unlike most Greek priests and priestesses, the Pythia did not inherit her office through noble family connections. Although the Pythia had to be from Delphi, she could be old or young, rich or poor, well educated or illiterate. She went through a long and intense period of conditioning, supported by a sisterhood of Delphic women who tended the eternal sacred fire in the temple. The Classical Explanation: Tradition attributed prophetic inspiration of the powerful oracle to geologic phenomena: a chasm in the earth, a vapor that rose from it, and a spring. Roughly a century ago scholars rejected this explanation when archaeologists digging at the site could find no chasm and detect no gases. The ancient testimony, however, is wide spread, and it comes from a variety of sources: historians such as Pliny and Diodorus, philosophers such as Plato, the poets Aeschylus and Cicero, the geographer Strabo, the travel writer Pausanias, and even a priest of Apollo who served at Delphi, the famous essayist and biographer Plutarch. Strabo [B.C.-A.D. 25] wrote: “They say that the seat of the oracle is a cavern hollowed deep down in the earth, with a rather narrow mouth, from which rises a pneuma [gas, vapor, breath; hence our words “pneumatic” and “pneumonia”] that produces divine possession. A tripod is set above this cleft, mounting which, the Pythia inhales the vapor and prophesies.” Plutarch [A.D. 46-120] left an extended eyewitness account of the workings of the oracle, He described the relationship among god, woman and gas by likening Apollo to a musician, the woman to his instrument and the pneuma to the plectrum with which he touched her to make her speak. But Plutarch emphasized that the pneuma was only a trigger. It was really the preconditioning and purification [certainly including sexual abstinence, possibly including fasting] of the chosen woman that made her capable of responding to exposure to the pneuma. An ordinary person could detect the smell of the gas without passing into an oracular trance. Plutarch also recorded a number of physical characteristics about the pneuma. It smelled like sweet perfume. It was emitted 'as if from a spring' in the adyton where the Pythia sat, but priests and consultants could on some occasions smell it in the antechamber where they waited for her responses. It could rise either as a free gas or in water. In Plutarch's day the emission had become weak and irregular, the cause, in his opinion, of the weakening influence of the Delphic oracle in world affairs. He suggested that either the vital essence had run out or that heavy rains had diluted it or a great earthquake more than four centuries earlier had partially blocked its vent. Maybe, he continued, the vapor had found a new outlet. Plutarch's theories about the lessening of the emission make it clear that he believed it originated in the rock below the temple. A traveler in the next generation, Pausanias, echoes Plutarch's mention of the pneuma rising in water. Pausanias wrote that he saw on the slope above the temple a spring called Kassotis, which he had heard plunged underground and then emerged again in the adyton, where its waters made the women prophetic. Plutarch and other sources indicate that during normal sessions the woman who served as Pythia was in a mild trance. She was able to sit upright on the tripod and might spend a considerable amount of time there [although when the line of consultants was long, a second and even a third Pythia might have to relieve her. She could hear the questions and gave intelligible answers. During the oracular sessions, the Pythia spoke in an altered voice and tended to chant her responses, indulging in wordplay and puns. Afterward, according to Plutarch, she was like a runner after a race or a dancer after an ecstatic dance. On one occasion, which either Plutarch himself or one of his colleagues witnessed, temple authorities forced the Pythia to prophesy on an inauspicious day to please the members of an important embassy. She went down to the subterranean adyton unwillingly and at once was seized by a powerful and malignant spirit. In this state of possession, instead of speaking or chanting as she normally did, the Pythia groaned and shrieked, threw herself about violently and eventually rushed at the doors, where she collapsed. The frightened consultants and priests at first ran away, but they later came back and picked her up. She died after a few days. The New Tradition: Generations of scholars accepted these accounts. Then, in about 1900, a young English classicist named Adolphe Paul Oppe visited excavations being carried out by French archaeologists at Delphi. He failed to see any chasm or to hear reports of any gases, and he published an influential article in which he made three critical claims. First, no chasm or gaseous emission had ever existed in the temple at Delphi. Second, even if it had, no natural gas could produce a state resembling spiritual possession. Third, Plutarch's account of a Pythia who had a violent frenzy and died shortly afterward was inconsistent with the customary description of a Pythia sitting on the tripod and chanting her prophecies. The temple has a number of anomalous features that would call for some special interpretation of its function even if the reports of Plutarch and others had not been preserved. First, the inner sanctum is sunken, lying two to four meters below the level of the surrounding floor. Second, it is asymmetrical: a break in the internal colonnade accommodates some now vanished structure or feature. Third, built directly into the foundations next to the recessed area is an elaborate drain for spring water, along with other subterranean passages. Thus, the temple of Apollo seemed designed to enclose a particular piece of terrain that included a water source, rather than to provide a house for the image of the god, the normal function of a temple building. During that first exploration, we traced the major east-west fault line, called the Delphi fault, that de Boer had observed during the earlier survey. Later we were to discover the exposed face of a second fault in a ravine above the temple. This second line, which we named the Kema fault, ran northwest southeast and cut across the Delphi fault at the oracle site. A line of springs that ran through the sanctuary and intersected the temple marked the location of the Kerna fault below the ancient terracing and the accumulated debris from rockslides. An Unexpected Inspiration: Two thousand years ago Plutarch was interested in reconciling religion and science. As priest of Apollo, he had to respond to religious conservatives who objected to the notion that a god might use a fluctuating natural gas to perform a miracle. Why not enter the woman's body directly? Plutarch believed that the gods had to rely on the materials of this corrupt and transitory world to accomplish their works. God though he was, Apollo had to speak his prophecies through the voices of mortals, and he had to inspire them with stimuli that were part of the natural world. Plutarch's careful observations and reporting of data about the gaseous emissions at Delphi show that the ancients did not exclude scientific inquiry from religious understanding. The primary lesson we took away from our Delphic oracle project is not the well-worn message that modern science can elucidate ancient curiosities. Perhaps more important is how much we have to gain if we approach problems with the same broad-minded and interdisciplinary attitude that the Greeks themselves displayed. Only surviving depiction of the priestess, or Pythia, at Delphi from the time the oracle was active reveals the low-ceilinged chamber and the Pythia seated on a tripod. In one hand she holds a sprig of laurel [Apollo's sacred tree]; in the other, a cup, presumably containing water from a spring that bubbled up into the chamber, bringing with it gases that induced a trance. This mythological scene shows King Aegeus of Athens questioning the first Pythia, Themis. An Athenian potter made the cup in about 440 B.C. Experiments with anesthesia conducted by Isabella Herb [standing] in the mid - 20th century turned out to be crucial in solving the mystery of what gas might have been emitted beneath the temple at Delphi. Herb and her colleagues had discovered that low concentrations of ethylene could produce a trance like state. By John R. Hale, Jelle Zeilinga de Boer, Jeffrey P. Chanton and Henry A. Spiller August 2003 Scientific American pages 67 to 73. <note: 3:37 P. M. Saturday August 14, 2004, day one of The Olympic Games>>. Go To page 89. Notice the different hand positions of the "two" statues of Mery. So the statues could be said to be seated upon either the base or flatten top of a pyramid. But the "door" to the pyramid is on one of the faces which is a simple form of an triangle. Back to page 97. Notice the darkness behind the statute <Block Statute and Niche Stela of Sahathor>. What is in the upper chamber of The Great Pyramid? A stone block to sit upon I believe? And what else? So what goes on all four in the morning and by two in the midday, and by three in the evening? Go To page 128. Look at the "Statuette of Thutmosis IV". Go to page 170. What is that upon the head of the "Cosmetic Vessel Held by a Girl"? Is that a box? And what is that upon the head of the "Bottle in the Form of a Female Lute Player". Is that a cup? But what is it about the middle sections of these figures? They do look rather "plump"! Hurry, go to page 187. Look at the "Mendicant Statue of Peraha". Read the commentary if you want, but remember the transitions. Go to page 196. What is that in the center of the drawing? Oh, it is a "lake". It is a "artificial lake surrounded by trees. The artists has emphasized the ambiguity of this setting with an extraordinary detail: a grapevine at the corner of the lake." Now look at page 197. The "Book of the Dead, Papyrus of Ani". "Book of the Dead, Papyrus of Ani: The Funeral Procession: FromThebes: New Kingdom, Nineteenth Dynasty [ca. 1295-1186 B.C.] Papyrus, painted; <excerpt> Ani was a scribe, whose titles indicate that he specialized in accounting. The three sections in this catalogue from his funerary papyrus [see also cat. nos. 102, 103] give only a taste of this amazing work, the total length of which is some 78 feet [almost 24 meters], with every vignette beautifully painted. It is perhaps the finest and certainly the best preserved of the Books of the Dead that have polychrome vignettes. This sheet shows Ani's funeral procession as it moves toward his tomb, where it will be met by grieving women and where the coffin will be stood erect for the last rites and the widow's last farewell before being taken into its final resting place. As on catalogue number 99, the writing of the long spell below is retrograde. Here, however, the backward writing presumably had a magical meaning <note>. Two pairs of oxen, guided by four men, haul the sledge bearing the coffin, which is preceded by a priest in a leopard-skin vestment [cf. cat. no. 55]. He turns back toward the coffin, to wave an incense burner and pour liquid from a tall libation vase. The large bier has the prow and stern of a boat, like the boat in which the sun god traveled across the sky. Large formal bouquets and statuettes of Nephthys and Isis flank the head and the foot of the anthropoid coffin, which is evidently on public display during its slow, final journey." We won't go into all of the scenes in the "Book of the Dead". Just to refresh ourselves, let's return to page 115. The statute of "Ptahemsaf". What is the story behind this kilt? Go to page 241. The "Standing Figure of Amenhotep holding a Naos". Go to page 253. What is that in the box of "Semathawy Holding a Naos"? And the Phoenix is said to give birth to his own self! Now can you figure out the meanings of the "Coffin of a Woman" on page 208? The Egyptians science was about immortality. And in this science they dealt with the seed of immortality born within the human body which grows into the immortal <immutable> body! Answer to the riddle: page 91 and analyze the writing, sekhem, scepter: it's a paddle for your boat, it's a till for the ground, it is a spade to beat the ground <the running of the serpents, the congo snake with legs <verses the frankenfish>, the electric eel>, the

bakers <I don't know what it is called, but you remove pizza from the stone oven with it, <spade> <see Egyptian Kundalini Sexual Tantra>>, the ax to split the wood, the grabbing of the serpent of the spine from the rear, the bakers mixing rod which leaves only the staff. <note: there are many ways to say the same thing when speaking about an event. Think of the words "sexual intercourse". Asked 1000 people to explain it. How many answers will you get?> The Hidden Master <even hidden from his own self, woooo>! Well, who is the
hidden master? Don't be confused. The Hidden Master is not the same as The Master in Hiding. The Hidden Master is the many <few> ones that travel the same path that leads to the next life, And Make It! First you learn <sit down>, then you think about what you learned, then you do! I came, I saw, I did it or conquered. First you know nothing. Then you think you know everything. Then you ask: "what is that?" Which one came first, the chicken or the egg? 6:43 a.m. Thursday February 26, 2004.

SIMPLE CIPHER ANSWER

The simple answer goes like this. A man goes into his lab of an unknown number of walls. He is gone for some time. When he comes out, he says that he has discovered a formula. People go in to see what it is that he has found. To their astonishment there are thousands of chalk boards filled with terms and scribble. There are notes everywhere. There are pieces of chalk all over the place. You get the idea. Some of the terms used on the boards they know, while others look like the writing of a baby. The man returns to the room. Everyone is silent. After a while, the man asks them what they think about his work. The room remains silent. The man says "oh I see"! He then writes on the floor in big letters: "E = m c(squared)". The kundalini science was the proof of the soul and inner garment called the second or inner body. The spirit self so to speak. This was a science that the Egyptians said was given to them by "THEE AMEN". This was the God of the gods. This was not the sun, but called THE SUN GOD. This God had control over the course of the solar sphere called RA which is our sun. Hence, they called him "THEE AMEN RA". In modern day he is biblically known to some as THE LORD. He left a record of his power over the elements in Isaiah 38:7-8. Want to here a joke? Isaiah could be ciphered as "Is ia ha" as in is funny. Ah, as in he has a sense of humor <4-16-2010-8:50>

LAST COMMENT

It is like traveling through dark deep space in a worm hole listening to the binaural remix of "In Your Wildest Dreams" by Tina Turner & Barry White on a mental plane, just breaking the known speeds of light while the ship vibrates to the Mariah Curey classic remix of "Honey". Right. Blackhole!

P. S. ESCAPE

Now, you wouldn't be trying to escape and live forever would you? You know like in the movies Stargate and Event Horizion <hori zion – The Matrix <matrix also means womb>>? You <you are> so funny! Could Egypt have been the grave yard of them waiting to be resurrected? The Book Of The Dead, why would the dead need a book like that also called Coming <coming – the urban dictionary> Fourth By LIGHT!

THE EGO

Some say that the ego can be a terrible thing. It can cause a person to act in a certain distasteful manner. Don't you just hate those types of people? You would think that they would learn to be humble. The bible even speaks about the ego.

I once saw a candid camera show where they played a trick on people. First, the person would be talking to one police officer. Some construction workers would walk between the officer and the person. That is when the scene would change. Sometimes there would be two officers. Sometimes they would exchange the male officer for a female. The skits went on and on. Then, I recall that Dr. Joyce Brothers explained the reaction of the people. She explained that when someone sees something that they do not understand, the mind will tell the conscience that they did not see what they thought that they saw. This is a mental protection device provided by the ego. The ego defines who the person is. The ego can be shattered by being confronted by what it cannot understand. That is said to be able to cause serious mental damage.

TO THEM THAT KNOW ME

I know some of you are going to be real happy for me. But I do know that some who know me are going to hate on me. I am having a Tupac Shakur moment of "picture me rolling! A select few might even utter the words 'oh no"! If they listen real carefully, they might hear the sounds of laughter. It is not good to get caught out there for playing around with The Christians! This is just not a good position to be in.

KUNDALINI ENERGY SYSTEM

Let us try to look at the human kundalini system as some kind of electro-magnetic system. First, we start with the two side paths of Ida and Pingala. We can think of them as magnetic poles. One would be north, while the other would be the south pole on a bar magnet. This bar magnet concept is the basis of the automobile alternator. It could be thought of as if Ida and Pingala phase their electro-magnetic energy into the root chakra. Using the seven color chakra system, we could think of sushumna as a type of filter or prism. It could be thought of as a type of string that has seven tap points. Each tap point gathers energy of a certain frequency range. These ranges relate to the seven light frequencies shown when white light goes through a prism. The seven points are called chakras. The seven chakras each have a color. These colors relate to different frequencies of light. The chakras could be thought of as gated capacitors.

The kundalini system could be thought of as a seven way speaker musical crossover system. What the kundalini exercise does is to reverse the separation process, thereby causing the energy of the seven colors to be pumped backward into the cord or line called sushumna. As the energy flow is reversed, the colors begin to mix back towards their original state. That state being white light. As the colors mix, they give off their magnetic charge. This charge saturates Ida and Pingala with negative and positive current. The filtered charge flows upward in "hidden ducts" to the jaws of the mouth. This path reaches beyond the medulla oblongata, or what is called the oblong gate. When the "yogi" or student starts the process, they lock or seal the body. One lock is at the neck, while the other is at the root chakra. It should be noted that the root chakra should be "charged" or primed before the whole process is started. This is done by the techniques given in "Kunddlini Sexual Tantra". The production of white light starts at the lowest point called red chakra. Energy flow is now disrupted from central line sushumna of the body. This causes the body to go into what could be called "the mystical coma" state. It is at this point that the body "dies". The heart does not stop beating because there is still energy in the body. The body begins to seal itself from the outside world. If one is in the yoga lock posture when this happens, something strange will take place. The eyes will seal shut. The ear drums will seal shut making the electric sounds of the brain very audible. The nasal pathways which control the fuel rate to Ida and Pingala will collapse shut. The jaws will lock with such pressure that the teeth will feel like hard sponges. It should be noted that this could crack several teeth. It appears that this action stimulates the nerves in "all" of the teeth which sends strange energy into the tongue. This causes the tongue to rise up like The Great Pyramid and move wildly about its sockets, if you will. The tongue dances in the mouth like a wild serpent closed in a hollow or cave. Remember that the external breathing system has been suspended. In other words, one cannot take in external air. I think this is the point of the great danger that is often spoken of. Who knows what will happen if one panics at this point? This is why the yogi's practice breathing or breath control. Just to give an example, the yogi might be placed in a sealed area that contains one hour worth of air. The yogi might not be released for three hours. The yogi has to control their breathing to use less oxygen while being in a sensory deprivation environment. This sensory deprivation may make the three hours seem like days or years. That is why the yogi master may play games with their own minds. A game might be the continuous adding of numbers starting from one plus one. There are thousands of games that the yogi could play to keep themselves calm during their "time travel". This is the point where one becomes short of breath so to say and panic can really set it. Oxygen, or prana is drawn or returned to the lungs via the yogis reverse breathing. In other words, it is as if oxygen is returned to the lungs from the body to fuel the most essential functions. This could be thought of as a rerouting the oxygen from other parts of the body back to the lungs. The toes and fingers do not need the oxygen that they store. The body is in an emergency state like being under an ice covered pond. The drama is unfolding. The electro-magnetic energy of the body is reversed also. It is sent into the root chakra via the nerves. The spine tingles as if ants were moving through it. These are electrical pulses. There is no reason that they body should be shutting down! It becomes an emergency situation for "the self"!

You know that blood cells do things to help seal and heal the damaged human unit. It appears that there is also an electro-magnetic emergency system in the human body. Think of it as an emergency electro-magnetic reboot system. It would be like priming the electrical fence in the movie Jurassic Park. It would be like the terminator rebooting in the Terminator movie. This is where the carducess symbol comes into play. There are several images of the carducess symbol. Each of the symbols that I have seen that are different say a different thing about the same subject. Some carducess symbols only have one snake. This would imply that only one nadis channel is open. That means that either Ida or Pingala is active. This is where the skill of the yogi comes into play. When in a state like that, it is implied that the yogi is going to have to use their mental power to weave the kundalini about the chakras on the "tree of life". One might say that the yogi was not purified enough to use the central path. To put it another way, the way or path was not made straight. This is where they say that the kundalini has to burn its way through the path upon the tree of life.

Remember in the writings on the subject, each chakra has its own drama based upon its color level. These dramas can cause trouble for the yogi. Let us say that the yogi makes it through the dramas to the neck lock. Remember the neck is locked via the chin to the chest position. This restricts fluid from traveling to and from the brain. The system knows that there is the fluid of life in the body and begins to "mine" for it. The hidden pathways of Ida and Pingala open via suction of the jaws. The paths extend from the two sides of the jaws down to the testies. The tongue opens the central pathway by boring a hole into the roof of the mouth. This is called "opening the hood of RA".

I have to add this to the discussion. I had felt for a long time that something was wrong about what was wrong about what was written about the kundalini opening process. Many people had written upon the subject. I feel very confident in saying that I don't think they know what they are talking about. The cipher key that I had was called The Apocalypse Unsealed by James M. Pryse. It appears that this work was published in 1919. It referred to an esoteric interpretation of the initiation of Ioannes. It went into great detail on the subject of kundalini science. What it did not do was to say what the kundalini opening process was, nor how to do it. So, you study to try to find out as much about the subject as you can. It is funny to look at what I consider to be the false information about "the bolt of brahma nadi <Brahmarandhra which is said to be "hollow of (or entrance to) Brahman" in some works>. From there, they might talk about cutting the base of the tongue with a knife a little at a time for weeks. Some talk about the kundalini rising up into the head for six months. All this here and that there type of stuff. First of all, they don't understand that the wings on the carducess symbol represent "the sphenoid bone" sometimes called "the wings of Hermes". I believe the error came from trying to interpret the writings called The Hatha Yoga Pradipika by Svami Svatmarama. It is said to have been written in 1400's A.D. from some older texts. It is said to have been translated in 1915. I think the Kechari <khechari> mudra" part of the text is written in code.

Great reverse pressure is inside of the sealed mouth. There is the great suckling like a baby upon the jaws. This radically increases the negative pressure in the mouth. The jaws tighten further which increases the nerve pressure upon the teeth. The tongue breaks through the upper pallet or roof of the mouth with a loud “crack”. It is like the sound from the movie Total Recall when the bug implant was removed. The sound is worst because it is heard from the inner ears because they are sealed shut. This is called “opening the hood of RA”. Ida and Pingala begin to flood the mouth with their respective fluids. The prostrate pump unit begins to flow in reverse. The spine or sushumma becomes pressurized. This is why Kundalini Sexual Tantra is so important. One needs enough fluid in the testies to pressurize each of the three pathways. Once the central pathway is pressurized and the tongue breaks through, the oblong gate opens. The jaws are still suckling, but now on the three ways or paths. Because there is great negative pressure in the mouth, the hole in the roof of the mouth begins to seep fluid. This causes the brain to move down. Because the chest oblong gate lock has released, this allows fluid to be drawn out of the prostrate mixer up the spine into the skull or cup. The brain/spine unit moves up and down like a well pump to draw more fluid into the skull cavity. This releases the lock on the red “active” chakra holding the kundalini. Remember that the inner body is in a blackout state. There is no inner light. Then there is the sound of great rushing water. This is the straight path. Where is this running water sound coming from? Do not panic, the yogi might say to themselves. Look, way, way, far away there is a light about the size of the head of a pen. There is something strange about the light says the yogi to themselves. It is moving at a very fast rate of speed. It is moving real fast. The light gets bigger, bigger. The light is spinning like a tornado! The light is white, red, and blue! What is that? White from the white light blend of the seven chakras. Red from the poking chakra place of the kundalini. Blue from the crossing over to the higher frequency chakras after the green chakra. What is that image? Is that the face of the moon? No! The yogis say that they saw a “serpent”. A serpent? Like a snake? No, they said a serpent! How about a happy white, red, and blue “dragon” with whiskers! Just as the yogi may think to themselves “dragon”, bam; the yogi gets hit in the third “seeing’ eye like Decond Frost in the movie Blade at the temple ritual. This is where the kundalini has “eaten” the mystical seed. The whole inner head goes pure white or bright silver gray as the sound of thunder is heard. The massive amount of white light energy travels from "the third eye" through the acupuncture circuits in one wave. This exposes the vision of the inner garment or spirit self.

After that part of the drama is complete, the brain reboots itself. Energy is sent to each part of the brain as if to clean the lines and give that area a hot shot. The parts of the brain fire as like from a distributer in a car. The individual sequential stimulation is said to be felt by the yogi. At a certain point the nerve area is zapped that controls an arm or a leg. That is when it is said that the yogi's practice of postures becomes of value. The restart of one of the legs might cause that leg to contort over ones head from behind. The arms might do the same. The yogi might be lead through a sequence of postures until the drama is over.

Wow, the end. Now it is time to relax. As the yogi goes to the bathroom, they may be meditating on the meaning of the exercise. The yogi may be in for a big surprise! Wow, front to back; not side to side! Wow! And so ends that which some call The Great Work. The next level is to understand what was done. This is a record of such a thing. Hotep is "to know"! There is a difference between believing and knowing. A believer can be fooled, but a knower cannot. The knower can only play at being the fool by transgression. Where does the dram begin? At the beginning of course. What would be the motto or cause effect of the doctrine?" "Now that you have done all that you know how to do, go back and read your bible from cover to cover! Wow!

WHAT

11-26-10

Ok. Alright. Let me write down the thought so that I can see it. Once I see it, then I shall perceive it. Once I perceive it, I shall use my perception to interpret what I am seeing. Then I shall try to understand what it is that I am questioning its meaning. First, let me say this: there are a lot of people who talk a lot and do not know what they are talking about. Then there is the group of people that do not talk about what they know. Then there are those that know a lot about part of a certain subject. Let me move on.

The topic of this thought is what is the Bible. The Wikipedia Encyclopedia says The Bible (from Greek τὰ βιβλία *ta biblia* "the books") is the various collections of sacred scripture of the various branches of Judaism and Christianity. Alright then, let me slow down. The Bible is what? A long sequence of words that have a meaning. The Bible is a long sequence of English characters that create words in the English language. The sequence of letters is the sequence of letters. If I think of the value of Pi, then there can only be one sequence of characters that define Pi. The same should be true for the Bible. If that is true, then why is there more than one version of the Bible? So, I conclude that each version of the Bible says "something" different no matter how small.

Now, we need to take a trip. I went to this place before. I was looking for a book.

We need to slow down. We have the Bible written in the English language. There are several versions. The Old Testament was written in the jewish language of hebrew. The New Testament and The Book of Revelation were written in the greek language. The three major books were translated into the latin language. From that, the Bible was translated into english by the authority of King James. The Rosetta Stone is an Ancient Egyptian granodiorite stele inscribed with a decree issued at Memphis, Egypt in 196 BC on behalf of King Ptolemy V. The decree appears in three scripts: the upper one is in Ancient Egyptian hieroglyphs, the middle one in Egyptian demotic script, and the lower text in Ancient Greek. Because it presents essentially the same text in all three scripts (with some differences between them), it provided the key to the modern understanding of Egyptian hieroglyphs.

One important concept is that Jesus of the Bible, the New Testament in particular, was said to have spoken in parables. This means that his statements could be interpreted in more than one way. One way was by what had already been said and happened in the scriptures. Another was by what had not happened, but was predicted in the scriptures. Then there is the way to interpret what he was saying by the worldly meaning versus the spiritual. It should be noted that Jesus was said to have spoken in Aramaic. That seems a little strange. Well, maybe that is not so strange compared to some other things in the text.

Other things like what? I am glad that you asked.

Here is a few:

1. The talking donkey <the television show, The Talking Mr. Ed>
2. The sun moving backward
3. the virgin birth <the existence of homophidites>
4. the rock boundary that moved behind the Israelites
5. the cloud by day and pillar of fire by night that lead the Israelites
6. the dead man that came back to life in the Old Testament
7. the concept of demons jumping into people <the movie Fallen and the exorcism series> While these movies are fiction, they are based upon real biblical concepts.
8. the biblical ship that Elijah is said to have been drawn up in. <The Mothership of the musical group Parlament Funkadelic>
9. the statement that an altar was built upon the center of the Earth. <the concept of the positioning of The Great Pyramid of Giza. The Giza complex is said to have been laid out based upon the pattern of the stars. In the Charlton Heston version of The Ten Commandments movie we see Moses using a building tool to mark the rise of a certain star on a certain day. In studying this form of architecture, I was led to a certain book. I asked for the book. When the librarian tried to retrieve it, she asked me how did I know about the book. I thought that was very strange, so I asked her what did she mean. She explained how the book was not categorized. She explained that a person would have to be looking for that exact book to find it. Anyway, I could not get the book until the next day.

I made other use of my time. The book described how Washington, D.C. was supposed to be laid out based upon The Sun, The Moon and the motion of the planets. How strange is that and why would an architect do such a thing? Wait, I recall a fellow named Le Font was supposed to be the architect. I recall that he left in the middle of the project. Then I recall that Benjamin Banneker finished the project. Wait! Benjamin Banneker was a negro. Negro, black, colored, darkie, whatever. Now history wants to enter the concept of not only was a negro of basic intelligence, but this negro was of the highest architectural order. They call him "The Man Who Saved Washington" and "An Early American Hero". Well, who forgot to mention that? You see now that the whole drama is becoming strange. For example, in the study of current day "metaphysics", it was stated that Egypt was not supposed to be in Africa which is why the Egyptians were not "black" people. The idea was proposed that you should call an airline and tell them that you want to go to Africa. Then, when they ask where in Africa, you respond with Egypt. I did just that and listened to the response of "Oh, you do not want to go to Africa, you want to go to Egypt". Say what and huh? It was the classic case of metaphysics strikes again. What kind of fool am I supposed to be? They, the editorial them, think that I am so dumb that I do not know that Africa is a continent. I wondered what other type of factual lies were roaming around out there?

Well here is a few:

1. Santa Claus
2. flying reindeer
3. a female angel on top of the Christmas tree or pagan may pole
4. a rabbit's relationship to Easter <the rabbit is a fertility sign due to its sexual nature and if you place a rabbi, like Jesus was, on a upright cross or "T", then you can spell the word "rabbi t">.

Wow, metaphysics strikes again. Let us not forget how it was taught at one time that the Earth was flat! They did so say that. That is why Christopher Columbus was so special. Not because shake and sphere are in the Bible, but because they forgot to mention the part about he and his brother were locked up when they returned from their trip due to "double dipping". They were supposed to have gotten money from Spain and Portugal. What about the "Blackmoors" or Moors of Spain? Who are they? While we are on Spain, there is a statue of Christopher Columbus in

Spain pointing to the new world. Well, I ask you, where did Christopher Columbus set foot upon the new world? The information I have says he did not get off of the boat. How can you find a new land with inhabitants upon it? That is what the South American Indians said: "How?"

Back to The Bible. Let us approach this from a different way. The first five books of the Old Testament are called The Torah. There are several different English versions of them. I read a few. The version I liked the best was supposed to have been translated by a group of rabbis that only wrote what they saw. I liked that. It is called The Stone Edition.

Alright! We will move to the obvious starting point which is the beginning of the book. No, not the New Testament; but the first book of the Torah. Of the Old Testament of the Bible! The first word of Genesis is a bible code. You might say "in the beginning". The word is Bereshith or something like that. I say that because I have seen it spelled several ways. Do you happen to notice a four letter root in the word? Metaphysics strikes again.

At this point I shall make reference to one numerical coding system that is called concordance. This book gives a numerical value for each word of the Bible. I just want to throw this concept in at this point. How many letters are there in the English alphabet? How many of them can you find by street name in Washington, D.C? Why is that? Metaphysics strikes again! So there is code number for the first word of the Bible. Did you notice that the first letter is "B"? Why is that? Now, we are moving into concepts of them whom are called Cabbalists or Kabbalists. Have you ever heard of the Kabbala or the Zohar? I have read them also. The Kabbalists have several different coding systems. One code breaks each letter of a word down into further letter codes. Another code gives a coded meaning or statement to each letter of a word. Then, we come to a concept put forward by a master kabbalist that each hebrew letter is generated by a single shape that fits inside of the human hand in a certain way. His name is Stan Tenen. It could be said that each letter could be expressed as a particular hand posture. These postures when connected together could cause the human body to form a "specific" dance similar to Tai Chi. I have heard it said that the mind has a type of grid that lets the mind know where the hand or finger is at all times and even in the dark.

We now speak of the human unit as being left or right handed. In the Tai Chi systems, the human body is ambidextrous. It is also said that the human form in Tai Chi is hard and soft which can relate to male and female. This male and female, or left and right could relate to the human thinking pattern. Why should someone be a left or right side of their brain thinker? Would an octopus favor one arm or tentacle? This concept relates to the said charter of the original Adam of the Bible. He or it was created him, her, them. Its name was Adam Kadmon. I conclude that its eye or brain was as one unit. And so, I conclude that this is also what the Bible is about. It is a tool that can be used to create a certain thinking pattern. From this thought pattern, the user can polarize the spirit body towards a next place called “the afterlife”. It is said that some people with “near death” experiences tell of visions during that time. What they generally are talking about is “the path”. In most cases, they are upon a sudden ride that they had not prepared for. That is not the case for the biblical student. The biblical student is prepared for a transition of reality that is reached through a mystical ride that takes them from the dimension of the earthly living to another dimension of their choice not default. The transition to the desired place might be called the transition of the mystical butterfly. The transition to the place of default might be called the transition of the moth. It is written that so as a man thinks so is he. Hotep <which means knowledge>!

THE NEGROS TASK

A short time ago, in a place called America, there was a thing called slavery. The slaves were called “Negros”. It was noticed that while a few perished under the hard labor, a great number of them grew in mental, physical and spiritual strength. They were noted to sing and rhythmically move while under great stress. They were also observed to grow deeper into spiritual beliefs as the stress increased. They began to look and call for what might be termed “The Mother Ship”! One may laugh at that term, but the Bible states that Elijah was “drawn up” in what? *Wikipedia Encyclopedia* cite: http://en.wikipedia.org/wiki/Christopher_Coumbus says,

"Christopher Columbus (c. 31 October 1451-20 May 1506) was an Italian explorer, colonizer, and navigator from the Republic of Genoa, in northwestern Italy, whose voyages across the Atlantic Ocean led to general European awareness of the American continents in the Western Hemisphere. With his four voyages of exploration and several attempts at establishing a settlement on the island of Hispaniola, all funded by Isabella I of Castile, he initiated the process of Spanish colonization which foreshadowed general European colonization of the "New World".

Although Columbus was not the first explorer to reach the Americas from Europe (being preceded by the Norse led by Leif Ericson, the voyages of Columbus molded the future of European colonization and encouraged European exploration of foreign lands for centuries to come.

Columbus's initial 1492 voyage came at a critical time of emerging modern western imperialism and economic competition between developing kingdoms seeking wealth from the establishment of trade routes and colonies. In this sociopolitical climate, Columbus's far-fetched scheme won the attention of Isabella I of Castile. Severely underestimating the circumference of the Earth, he estimated that a westward route from Iberia to the Indies would be shorter than the overland trade route through Arabia. If true, this would allow Spain entry into the lucrative spice trade — heretofore commanded by the Arabs and Italians. Following his plotted course, he instead landed within the Bahamas Archipelago at a locale he named San Salvador. Mistaking the lands he encountered for Asia, he referred to the inhabitants as "indios" (Spanish for "Indians")."

So, if the people whom he found were not Indians, then who might they be in his mind? Them Nagas!

REAR COVER

Christian Kundalini Science. What is Christian Kundalini Science? It is a mental, physical and spiritual exercise found in The Bible. In specific, the key to it can be deciphered from The Book of The Revelation. The encyclopedia, *Wikipedia*, defines revelation in religion and theology, as revealing or disclosing through active or passive communication with supernatural entities (divine). It is believed that revelation can originate directly from a deity, or through an agent, such as an angel.

Here is how the term Christian Kundalini Science is formed. It is Christian because the cipher key clues are found in the Christian part of The Bible. The major clue is found at Revelation 13:18 as given by THE AMEN at Revelation 3:14. It should be noted that the science is referred to in The Old Testament. Kundalini is the core Hindu name for the science. One does not have to worry about using the Hindu version of the name because the science is polarized by the Christian spiritual book and what could be called The Christ Force. It is a science because it is an experiment that has a desired result listed at Revelation 3:12.

Stella 55001 is giving a hieroglyphic example of the Egyptian concept of how the kundalini is opened. The reason that the Egyptologist could not read it is because it is written in the secret sacred Egyptian priesthood language. I have told you now what it is. I do not think that it would be right to tell you exactly what the sequence says at this time. On the other hand, maybe I should. You do know that this is the knowledge of the pharaohs called The Nagas?

THE BEAST

What man in his right mind, and worldly experience would want to pass down his sorrows, lies, rumors, myths, fables, and misunderstandings to his children? He that does not mind to do such a thing is a beast, sadly enough; they will not know it!

ROULETTE

It would seem strange to think that the roulette wheel could be compared to the two wheels of the zodiac. According to roulettes Wikipedia page, “the sum of all the numbers on the roulette wheel (1 to 26) is 666, which is the ‘Number of the Beast’”. We can see a reflection of the two zodiac wheels in the fact that the French wheel has 37 slots while the American wheel has 38.

THE 13TH SYMBOL

Kundian and the "a man"!

[The Greatest Secret has to be "a/the" truth.] What is a/the truth? It might have to do with the/a meaning of Life! Truth is supposed to be knowledge. Knowledge is supposed to be "said" power. What kind of "power"?

CIPHER ROOT – COMPARE TO TRANSCRIPT

Where should I start with the cipher of stela 55001? What about if I start at the beginning of The Turin Erotic Papyrus. 00:00:18~It is a very rare example, because there aren't' all that many of that kind.

00:01:41 And I think that view of them is much more interesting than just seeing them as strange, exotic figures dominated by mummies, myths, magic and pyramids.

00:02:41 <key> In Italy, for example, the Popes decreed that all genitalia should be covered up with fig leaves. Why should they be ashamed, that is said to come with "the Popes decreed".

00:02:53 <<NARRATOR: One such example is the mutilated statue of Min, the Egyptian god of fertility, kept at the British Museum.

00:03:20 Min's penis could not be removed"!

00:03:37 ">>NARRATOR: Even today, some sexual images are kept hidden from the public. Close to where the Turin Erotic Papyrus was discovered on the West Bank of Thebes, there is an archaeological site, 3,000 years old, kept secret from thousands of visitors nearby."

"Would Hatshepsut be imaged as Isis like Cleopatra is said to be?"

00:06:56 "The laws of Mart"

00:07:08 "Similarities to one of the 12 positions"

00:08:16 "The walls are filled with hidden codes."

00:14:23 "Rebirth"

00:14:39 "The key word here is the lotus flower."

00:14:41 "The lotus flower is a symbol of resurrection."

00:15:15 "It did then as it does today."

00:15:52 "Codes"

0016:16 "Encoded message"

00:16:26 "The key to this clue is its double meaning"

00:16:29 "The word "seti" in Egyptian means "shooting," but it also means to ejaculate, which has very sexual significance because they wanted to be reborn in the hereafter, in the afterlife, and in order to be reborn, they had to have some sexual activity beforehand"

00:16:47 "And this is what is explained here in a coded message."

00:16:51 "And this is a way of visualizing this very vital sexual energy which they needed to be reborn."
>>NARRATOR: Hunting was a common metaphor for sexual prowess in the ancient world.

00:17:03 "Similar codes have been found on the tomb wall of an accountant named Nebamun"

00:17:54 ">>MANNICHE: It does show the 12 positions of intercourse" Hidden Rites

00:17:57 """Cummins : Only certain people would be able to come into this part of the temple, probably priests, not ordinary people who would be kept outside the temple precinct, so these images would be hidden and wouldn't be a part of what the everyday people would be seeing."

00:18:34 "Hieroglyph symbols provide clues that sex was important to the ancient Egyptian gods."

00:18:40 ">>DR. KELLY DIAMOND: The ancient Egyptians had two ways of writing their language, one of which was in hieroglyphics or sacred carved writings."

00:21:14 "The scene is a lot more coded than you would see in a tomb or maybe even a graffiti or whatnot, because it shows the gods. And so you don't have the image of Isis as a woman, you have an image of Isis shown as a kite or a bird of prey"

Key

00:21:41 "It's something that does show the power of Osiris through his phallus, and it was very important to show these two on a different level, than say the rest of the divinities or even the rest of the population at large."

00:22:21 "So the coded symbols and graphic depictions were not just a way to be reborn into the afterlife."

00:26:54 "NARRATOR: The Turin Erotic Papyrus offers a shocking-but- cryptic image of sex in ancient Egypt."

00:33:23 "But how did ordinary ancient Egyptians feel about sex?"

>>NARRATOR: We know that some sexual images are connected with the gods . . . and others with the rituals of fertility . . ."

00:39:42 "Narrator: It is now viewed as a microcosm of Egyptian society."

"MANNICHE: You would find people who were extraordinarily literate because they were scribes and artists, so compared to other villages all over Egypt, this is a very, very special place."

">>NARRATOR: The site has yielded a wealth of artifacts and texts that provide vital information about the way these people lived and how they viewed sex."

00:40:07 "This papyrus has survived from the late New Kingdom period in around 1500 BC."

00:40:13 "It reveals the sexual antics of an artisan."

00:44:41 "She has fingers like lotus flowers."

Key 2

00:49:35 "Yet its true meaning remains a mystery."

00:51:06 "Narrator: The severely damaged papyrus has not been treated well by time. Although sections are missing, there is enough fragmentary evidence to allow scholars to fill in this ancient jigsaw puzzle.

00:51:30 ">>PARKINSON: With something like the Turin Erotic Papyrus, it's very hard to know what it was used for."

00:51:48 "Some have suggested that it's a religious text."

"NARRATOR: On one section of the papyrus are images of animals imitating human behavior, which has left some scholars to believe that the papyrus is meant to be humorous."

One sequence shows a woman having sex on a chariot – a mysterious I mage scholars."

00:53:45	>>"Exell: We see images of scantily clad young ladies involved in the sexual act."
00:55:18	"We have 12 different positions of intercourse. Some would like to relate it to the world of the gods."

Key 3

00:55:44	"NARRATOR: One image shows a woman pleasuring herself on an ancient pot known as an amphora."
00:57:35	">>HUGHES: The priceless thing about this papyrus is that it allows you to decode real Egyptian sexuality."

GEMINI – THE TWINS

In the style of the zodiac, it is very important to understand the motion of "The Twins"! They can be very deceptive. They can act as one, two, or even three. They can mask themselves to act as many multiples. Their mother, the greater zodiac, can see their 12x12=144,000 motions; but when they become "unruly" <eclipsing>, it is hard to keep track of them. They are the twins. They can be very much the same, but causing a very different outcome upon the track of the zodiac. Hence, they wreck havoc. They, unchecked, can reach wear down the mother of the zodiac, the 12x12=144,000+1=145,000=1,000,000= zed of the lesser zodiac, zed of the greater zodiac, reset of the great grand zodiac. The ancient one – the need to awaken the ancient one - the one whom sleeps.

As the zodiac moves, they call him "father of time – the elder", his children become untamed by their circuits of time itself, as he left as a rule, their mother, the grand zodiac, cannot control their course upon the circuits. Their path wanders like the great stars called comets. His central eye opens to track the patterns from the core of the universe. He takes a breath in to number and rule the motions. His eyebrows bend at the disorder. His face quenches to see such a thing. His exhale moves the darkness of space to rest "The Order"! His frown shows the dislike of the back of order. His intensity calls for control. His meditative stare reaches out for order. His eye, eyes, eye, closes in a gesture of "and so it is done"! His children, the zodiac, set loose as by twins have been put in their place upon their course of their mother. The zodiac, by the Ancient One! The All Seeing I, The Master of the Zodiac, The Dark Core! <You do not want The Dark Core – that is the way out – where you have never been before – "Way Out" song by Steve Arrington – Oh!>

ESOTERIC OPENING

According to the symbolic opening of the chakras, the alpha man must control "his" microcosmic order of the macrocosmic zodiac and crisscross the "now" given firing order of the chakras to achieve the beta order. What is being said is that what happened due to Adam and Eve had knocked the firing order of the humans' Tree of Life out of order. The human engine still runs, but not to its higher order level. It is the human unit; wires are crossed so to speak. Hence, the planetary feeding pattern is out of alignment or order. This crossed pattern gives off what might be called a false Capricorn signal. The signal appears cosmically real, but it is not. It is like looking at a beam of light and not knowing that the path is bent due to the gravitational pull of an unseen body. The path of The Light is bent or arched! Hence, the seen path is not the shortest distance, nor is it a straight line. It could be called an optical illusion. When did man find out that light could bend?

This brings forth the "yoga" type male/female singular stable standing columer wave static opening of the chakras. It is like DJ Big Rel's Headbangerz volume fourteen, tracks ten through fourteen. Track ten is the prelude. Track eleven is the introduction. Track twelve is when the amplifiers open. Track thirteen is the jump off. Track fourteen is the stabilizer. This sequence might be followed by "Don't go lose it baby" by Hugh Masekela at 8 minutes long.! That might be called The Rush!

NEW THOUGHT

The Bible states at Genesis 2:24 that “Therefore shall a man leave his father and his mother, and shall cleave unto his wife: and they shall be one flesh”.

Mark 10:7 states that, “For this cause shall a man leave his father and mother, and cleave to his wife”.

Ephesian 5:31 states, “For this cause shall a man leave his father and mother, and shall be joined unto his wife, and they two shall be one flesh.”

They do not say anything about her leaving her father and mother. That also implies that the woman might not change traditions in her heart because of the man. I figured that one out long ago.

The new thought that I had I think was stimulated by a television show called “Gates of Hell”. My thought went like this: “If a man will leave his father and mother to cleave to his wife, what would that man be like if his wife was “caused” to leave him?” Noticed I used the term “caused”.

OUR FRIEND

Here we are with our friend, man, contemplating on what to do as he is in the safe guard of The Great Pyramid. Right outside of the pyramid lays in wait The Great Sphinx. It was the Sphinx that was to guard the way against ANYONE WHOM TRIED TO GATHER THE KNOWLEDGE OF The Great Pyramid. Why would there be such a thing? It has to do with “the fall of man” and the mixing with mankind.

Let me put that another way. It had to do with man believing a lie and man whom was created mixing his seed with them that came with creation. As the man lay contemplating his fate, he began to notice things about the pyramid do to “the teachings of the lights”. He learned about several lights.

The man found himself inside of the great cosmic classroom. He learned about the concepts of “as above, so below”. He began to learn about the sacred geometry. He learned about the concepts of the Nehushtan. All that was left was for him to choose by which path he would escape. He chose something that he had read in the stellar light. On the coffer top written in a special type of ink that was only visible inside of the pyramid, there was a passage on one of the pages that said "I am The Light, I am The Way"! The coffer top acted like a modern day computer tablet. You could turn the virtual pages to read more. The motion of the Earth also did something funny to the inside of The Great Pyramid. It caused the outer walls, not the casting stones, but the place in between to take on the holographic flat screen television appearance. This was not just one screen. It was several screens including up and down. You could say that the whole inner complex created <360 x 360=> 129,600 degrees of knowledge being taught at any given time. The images were not static like a wall painting. The images were dynamic like watching several television screens at one time in a holographic set. Our friend, the man, then made himself ready for his greatest work. What was that great work? It was to make it out of The Great Pyramid "alive". He had come from the east and traveled to the west. This led him to the face of The Sphinx. I have seen it written that The Sphinx's face is towards the east. Now, why would that be? Well, if The Sphinx is looking in the direction of the Sun, there would be a certain time that The Sphinx could watch the solar light move across the land towards it. But The Sphinx has two eyes? Yes, one to watch "the motion of the spheres" and the other to watch for they whom try to "pass". Ok, but The Sphinx is not a bird. Well, it is said to have wings. Well, suppose you were to approach at night when the sky was moonless, from the other side, while The Sphinx was crouching on the ground like it is now? Ok, yes, sure you could get upon The Great Pyramid's exterior; but how would you get/break in? That is a question that I had until February 16, 2011.

The Egyptians were into the stars. This is a known thing. No, no, no; let us start another way. It is night time. You and I are outside. It is thousands of years ago. There is nothing happening. We notice how some stars blink. We even try to see if there is a pattern to the stars blinking. You happen to know something about the stars. You point out and explain to me about the group of stars called "The Big Dipper". Wow! That is what the Egyptians did. They pointed out certain stars. Ok, so the star that aligns <the

entrance/exit> The Descending Path is said to be the Star of Huban, page 60, *Pyramidology Book* I by Adam Rutherford. Alright, I live a long way from The Great Pyramid, but I can see that star from where I live. What does that have to do with anything? Ah, nothing;' but it gives me food for thought. You do not want to walk up face to face with The Sphinx. There is that nasty tricky question. What about those teeth? If you answer the question, you now have to figure out how you are going to get inside of The Great Pyramid! Ok, I think that The Great Pyramid is the lost ancient light house. I write about this in other unpublished works. Think of The Great Pyramid as the reverse of a prism. Do you think that under certain conditions the reflection of The Sun would not appear "in the clouds"? There is a clue. How would the rising sun look with its own reflection upon it? How would the solar image change during the day? Would the solar image land upon more than one face of the eight pyramid faces? Could more than one reflection be seen in the sky at one time? Could sailors use The Sun and its reflection to sail to the trade place called Egypt in Africa? What type of image would be reflected upon the sky if The Sun was directly over top of The Great Pyramid? At any time of The Sun's solar transit would the reflection appear to be a triangle pointing the way to The Great Pyramid? What would you say if you saw that image in the sky? Would you think that someone is sending up a type of Bat Signal? Would the sign that moves upon the clouds by saying come here? What would the reflected image be if you consider the solar angle and the possible interference of the other pyramids? It could have been that the pyramid "complex" caused many images to be reflected in the sky! Upon seeing The Great Pyramid for oneself, would one ask themselves, "What is that?"

Here come the rest of the questions. Who built that? Why? How? For what? How? Why? What is that? As you follow the signs in the clouds, if you approach The Great Pyramid from the east or west you might notice something strange. At a certain point, you might see the mystical eye inside of The Sun. You might see the said "missing cap stone" appear. From the correct angle, you might see the top of the pyramid with the sun about half way above the pyramid's apex. At that moment, you might notice that you can see a small dark circular object or disk inside of The

Sun. Is that Ra's solar disk or ship? Is that the Egyptian sign of the circle with the dot in the middle? Is that the c s or cap stone? C s backward is sc. English is read left to right. Many ancient writings were read right to left. So s c could mean see as in "see the light". Suppose The Great Pyramid was intact. You play a game called "Move The Sphinx". You move The Sphinx statue to China. Do you think that The Sphinx would know how to "get home"? Yes, the directions would be in "the clouds". All The Sphinx would have to do is follow "the yellow pyramid bricked road to the land of Oz". Oz backwards is zo <zoo>. Where do you find the animals, so to speak? The zoo <has, ha, Ha>?

Anyway, you follow the signs in the sky towards The Great Pyramid. Suppose you're into that ancient bible thing. You might be on a quest to find The Garden of Eden. You recall what was said about "the mighty charbeum and a flaming sword that turned every which way?. Symbolically speaking, you have found "one". I say "one" because you could be wrong. So, you answer the question of The Sphinx. Now, you have to try to get inside of The Great Pyramid. Alright, you used the signs in the sky to get here. You're past The Sphinx. Now, what do you do? You think! You are in Egypt Africa. So? Who do you know that knows something about Egypt? Ah, Captain Kirk of the Star ship Enterprise! No! How about Moses of The Bible? Yes! But Moses "left" Egypt <P.S. I think Moses might have "blown" the inner seals in The Great Pyramid with the water turning to blood thing>. Do you know anybody whom went to Egypt, because they might know some secrets on how to get there? How about Jesus? Are not Jesus and Moses connected? When Jesus came was there said to be some kind of star that "the wise men" followed? Let us forget about the shafts stars because we have not gotten inside yet. So what stars might mean something to us? How about The Sun and the pole star? You guess that the ancient pole star Alpha Draconis (Dragon star) <The Great Dragon had been cast down into a bottomless pit> <This is key in one of my unpublished writings>. So now you have a vertical star line coming down the face of The Great Pyramid. From the Bethlehem line you can get another line on the pyramid face. <Draco star bible> Right here – sudden epiphany. It has to deal with my "Giza Trapezium Theory". Wow, it is out there. Let me finish this so you might use a stella angle and the Bethlehem line to guess at a "break in" point. Let us get back to our friend, the man, and his situation in the pyramid. The man has to learn all about the pyramid knowledge.

CIPHER CONFUSION

The traditional life-story [Tibetan: *namthar*] of **Niguma,** the female companion of Naropa, begins during the time of one of the earliest Buddhas in a region covered by water ruled by a great Naga King. This Naga was an accomplished and compassionate disciple of that Buddha and gave his permission for the miraculous drying up the water for the purpose of erecting a great temple and monastery. A bustling city grew up around these which acquired a certain reputation, and came to be called *The Land of Great Magic*. This is the place that Niguma was born.

Niguma developed the powerful tantric techniques referred to as the **Five Dharmas of Niguma**. The best known is called the ***Dream Yoga of Niguma***. Her disciple, **Naljor**, is considered the head of the **Shangpa Kagyu** denomination of Tibetan Buddhism.

TURIN EROTIC PAPYRUS

cite: http://fr-fr.facebook.com/note.php?note_id=167542506611647

Turin Erotic Papyrus

The Turin Erotic Papyrus (Papyrus 55001, also called the Erotic Papyrus or even Turin Papyrus) is a famous ancient Egyptian papyrus scroll-painting that was created during the Ramesside Period (approximately in 1150 B.C.Q. Discovered in Deir el-Medina in the early 19th century, it has been dubbed "world's first men's mag." Measuring 8.5 feet (2.6 m) by 10 inches (25 cm), it consists of two parts, one of which contains twelve erotic vignettes depicting various sex positions. It is currently held by the Museo Egizio in Turin, Italy.

Animal section

The first third depicts animals performing various human tasks. This part of the scroll-painting has been described as satirical and humorous.

Erotic section

Containing twelve successive scenes, the erotic section takes up two-thirds of the Turin Papyrus.

Not conforming the convention of bodily perfection in ancient Egyptian art, the men depicted on the papyrus are "scruffy, balding, short, and paunchy" with exaggeratedly large genitalia. In contrast, the women are nubile and appear with canonical erotic images of convolvulus leaves, Hathoric imagery, lotus flowers, monkeys and sistra. Overall, the artistic merit of the images is high, suggesting that the Erotic Papyrus had an elite owner and audience. The various male images have also been interpreted as a single protagonist, who has several encounters with a courtesan.

<*A> NO EASY WAY

There is no easy way to approach an image that you can see as a whole, and then to dissect it into parts. Hence, the cipher of "The Turin Stela Papyrus 55001".

The image shows me that it is talking about Kundalini Sexual Tantra right from first view. An internet search gives me some clues as to what the parts may be saying.

Nagas cite www.khandro.net/mysterioius_naga.htm:

The word Naga comes from the Sanskrit, and nag is still the word for snake, especially the cobra, in most of the languages of India. When we come upon the word in Buddhist writings, it is not always clear whether the term refers to a cobra, an elephant (perhaps this usage relates to its snake-like trunk, or the pachyderm's association with forest-dwelling peoples of northeastern India called Nagas,) or even a mysterious person of nobility. It is a term used for unseen beings associated with water and fluid energy, and also with persons having powerful animal-like qualities or conversely, an impressive animal with human qualities.

In WW II, learn how inhabitants of Nagaland land came to the world's attention.

Mythology

In myths, legends, scripture and folklore, the category naga comprises all kinds of serpentine beings. Under this rubric are snakes, usually of the python kind (despite the fact that naga is usually taken literally to refer to a cobra,) deities of the primal ocean and of mountain springs; also spirits of earth and the realm beneath it, and finally, dragons.

" ... every naga has a snake as its guardian deity. Fishing is prohibited in these springs, though the fish which come out of the main garbha [den, lair] of a nag can be caught. Restrictions on fishing have definitely helped to some extent to preserve water ecology."

Naga and Fertility

Because of its shape and its association with renewal, the serpent is a phallic symbol. This powerful emblem of fertility is thought to bring plentiful harvests and many children – images of nagas adorn houses and shrines and temples. It is said that when a king once banned snake worship, his kingdom suffered a drought, but the rains returned once the king himself placated Vasuki.

<*B)> SAID TO SYMBOLISUM

Erotic papyrus of Turin cite: www.egyptancient.net/erotic_papyrus.htm

EROTIC PAPYRUS OF TURIN

Probably written and illustrated by a painter from the Dair-El-Medina village, the papyrus is divided in two sections: the satiric one and the erotic one.

It goes back to the XX Dynasty (1186-1069 BC) it has in the satiric part, humanized animals, the comicality is based upon the overturn of the situations: the hawk tries to cub with a ladder, on a tree, where there is a hippopotamus; a for presided by cats is attacked by mice guided by a leader-mouse. The protagonist of the erotic part is a bearded man, with the peasants' short skirt, during the encounter with a courtesan, which is described with many details and a surprising sense of humor. Very famous, because one of its kind, it has always been kept in the Egyptian Museum in Torino. Discovered in the first years of 1800 it amazed a lot, giving an image of ancient Egypt, that loved life and pleasures. This papyrus tells about a moment of royal life: the Egyptian woman is preparing herself an erotic encounter, adding various elements such as the wig, flowers in her hair and putting on stake-up.

The lotus flower on the head had a particular symbol: the one of beauty and of desire. The jar, on which she was sitting, probably held ointments for hair and for intimate parts.

Jean-Francois Champollion, who saw it in Torino, in 1824, commented in his notes: “There were an image of monstrous obscenity that gave me a really strange impression about Egyptian wisdom and composure...”.

Egypt was in that time very open, with a sane erotic sense, love songs and lyrics, of course more refined, nevertheless had a sexual background and the women of could inherit, divorce, the had guarantees and rights.

Hippopotamus

Cats

Mice

Old man with beard

Short skirt during the <solar> encounter

CIPHER COLLISION

SYMBOLIC TURN

2 parts: 1) satiric, the other erotic
Satiric – humanized animals <like the god glyphs found in Egypt>
Erotic – there is "a bearded man. Royal life: the Egyptian woman is preparing herself for an erotic encounter' <spiritual might be said between father time and the queen of the zodiac. A meeting of the inner and outer circle or circulation to create the Grand Zodiac Motions of the twelve times twelve houses of the 144,000. The 144,000 zodiac unions with the three spheres of The Sun, The Earth, and The Moon to create the G. The G being a symbol for galaxy.

I had began to cipher multiple things at one time <*A> and <*B>. This way of looking at the picture is very hard to put into a coherent writing style – like the picture I might add. With that, I shall restart the cipher from an elemental perspective.

BIG PHALLUS

I would like to start with an image on the papyrus. There is the man under a sofa type of bed with the lotus woman on top. Now, why would he be under the bed unless it is symbolic? I introduce the term 'bier". *Wikipedia Encyclopedia* cite: http://en.wikipedia.org/wiki/Bier, says "a bier is a stand on which a corpse, or coffin or casket containing a corpse, is placed to lie in state or to be carried to the grave". (Reference: *The American Heritage Dictionary of the English Language* (American Heritage Publishing Co., Inc., New York, 1973), s.v., "bier")

In Christian burial, the bier is often placed in the center of the nave with candles surrounding it, and remains in place during the funeral.

The bier is a flat frame, traditionally wooden but sometimes of other materials. In antiquity it was often a wooden board on which the dead was placed, covered with a shroud. In modern times, the corpse is rarely carried on the bier without being first placed in a coffin or casket, though the coffin or casket is sometimes kept open.

A bier is often draped with cloth to lend dignity to the funeral service. The modern funeral industry uses a collapsible aluminum bier on wheels, known as a "church truck" to move the coffin to and from the church or funeral home for services.

Biers are generally smaller than the coffin or casket they support for reasons of appearance. As a result, they are not particularly stable, and can tip over unless well centered and undisturbed.

So, now we are talking about death rituals! It appears as if he is lying on a fully charged phallus. Not too bad for a looking upward dead man. This is about the upper and lower chambers, The Kings and Queens's chambers, if you will. At 00:56:14 of the transcript, we find the term "on top of an 'amphora'. 'She is obviously pleasuring herself oh this vase". The comment at 00:56:43 says: "You can just about read out.

She's kind of saying, "Come here, big boy, dirty boy, you kind of sex criminal." 00:56:44 "And he's obviously enjoying this moment, because he's got a huge engorged phallus which is resting just next to the amphora."

Right here is where we come to the fork in the road. 00:56:44 ">>NARRATOR: Ultimately, the evidence suggest the Turin Erotic Papyrus, 00:56:57 may be the world's oldest men's pornographic magazine".

No it is not! *Wikipedia Encyclopedia* cite: http://en.wikipedia.org/wiki/Amphora, says the word "amphora (plural: amphorae or amphoras) is a type of ceramic vase with two handles and a long neck narrower than the body. The word *amphora* is Latin, derived from the Greek *amphoreus* (αμφορεύς), an abbreviation of *amphiphoreus* (αμφιφορεύς), a compound word combining *amphi*- ("on both sides", "twain") plus *phoreus* ("carrier"), from *pherein* ("to carry"), referring to the vessel's two carrying handles on opposite sides". (Reference: Goransson, Kristian: *The transport amphorae from Euesperides: The maritime trade of a Cyrenaican city 100-250 BC*, Acta Archaeologica Lundensia, Series in 4o No. 25, Lund/Stockholm 2007, 9.) It is a vase with "two legs" and an unlided "womb"! It represents a woman whose womb has been "turned upside down". This is not a worldly text, but a coded spiritual text. The top of the pyramid is flat. The bottom of a vase or amphora is flat. By the lid being in the shape of a cone or cap stone, it implies that something of a higher order is taking place. A woman on a "cap stone" and all you can think about is animalistic sex? Why would not the woman remind you of Cleopatra, the Temple of Dandria whom hovers over the night sky? Does not the pyramid pierce the sky at night? Is not the pyramid the solar measure for the day?

Why would not the said twelve male/female positions remind one of the lesser/greater zodiacs? Why would lesser sexual encounters rage through your mind when you see zodiac animals dancing with joy as if it were the coming of the great year? What about a cipher of the term "pherein"? Take away the vowels you have "p, h, r, and n". Do you see a possible relationship to?

1) Phrenia
2) Phren
3) Phrenology,or
4) He-phern = 666 and so as a man thinks, so is he: the ego!>?

Wikipedia the term "MIN". Is he not a dead erect penis god? They are not talking about dead people or the Book of Life or The Book of the Dead. The Book is dual! In case if you do not do "The Great Work" in life, you still might have a chance!

So here is this Egyptian bearded <wise> guy running around with a huge phallus <Johnson>. What is that all about? *Wikipedia* the term "phallus'. Do you see the "Mural of Mercury in Pompeii"? Notice the tip <or head> seems to be "tied off". In the Chinese that is called 'drawing kung'. Does he look 'old' and/but sexually virile? His phallus looks bigger than the carduess' symbol behind his back! Why don't you Wikipedia "Ithyphallic"! What does the carducess coil have to do with this? Kundalini Sexual Tantra - the use and ability to draw "cosmic" sexual energy into the seven zodiacal chakras! What does the "swollen phallus' and the carducess coil have to do with this? The two create yin/yang so to speak. That is a standing columner. The foot wings imply upward motion. The curled chair implies spiral or vortex power. Hence, the whole image speaks of open kundalini power. Another cipher.

CONCLUSION

The Turin Papyrus 55001 is another coded graphic that has been handed down through time to "keep" the secrets of the zodiac openings of Man. On one hand, it looks very silly. It is as if it is of the most simple minded person's thoughts. That is just how it is supposed to look to the uninitiated!

IN CLOSING

They now in this age have many names for the identifiable transition points of the human being. In the current system, the reader might not be able to distinguish between the description of a male or female. To demonstrate this point, I use the term adolescent. Is that a girl or a boy? The Egyptian mind set used clues and symbols in respect to whom they were talking about in the male/female, mental/physical/spiritual orders. This is how Hathor could be said to be a Ra's mother, daughter, wife, and sky-goddess. The same was/is true for Ra-man. He went through several stages. He was a baby, a child, an adolescent, young adult, adult, husband, father, grandfather, and so on. In the end Ra was himself. The comment of Hathor would be: "and so; now I, mother Earth, the womb, the vessel, your vessel, your Queen, your universe; no longer has control of you because you are/have become your own Star. You A-Dam Right! Signed "ME"!

Wikipedia Encyclopedia cite: http://en.wikipedia.org/wiki/Hathor "Hathor had a complex relationship with Ra, in one myth she is his eye and considered his daughter but later, when Ra assumes the role of Horus with respect to Kingship, she is considered Ra's mother. She absorbed this role from another cow goddess 'Mht wrt' ("Great flood") who was the mother of Ra in a creation myth and carried him between her horns. As a mother she gave birth to Ra each morning on the eastern horizon and as wife she conceives through union with him each day. (Reference: a b e d e f g / Oxford Guide to Egyptian Mythology, Donald B. Redford (Editor), p157-161, Berkley Reference, 2003, ISBN 0-425-19096-X.)"

Hathor, along with the goddess Nut, was associated with the Milky Way during the third millennium B.C. when, during the fall and spring equinoxes, it aligned over and touched the earth where the sun rose and fell. (Reference: A Searching for ancient Egypt: art, architecture, and artifacts from the University of Pennsylvania Museum of Archaeology, and Anthropology, University of Pennsylvania. Museum of Archaeology and Anthropology, David P. Silverman, Edward Brovarski, p41, Cornell University Press, 1997, ISBN 0-8014-3482-3.) The four legs of the celestial cow represented Nut or Hathor could, in one account, be seen as the pillars on which the sky was supported with the stars on their bellies constituting the milky way on which the solar barque of Ra, representing the sun, sailed. (Reference: ^ The tree of life: an archaeological study, E. 0. James, p66, BRILL, 1967, ISBN 90-04-01612-0.) An alternate name for Hathor, which persisted for 3,000 years, was Mehturt (also spelt Mehurt, Mehet-Weren't, and Mehet-uret), meaning 'great flood, a direct reference to her being the milky way. [citation needed] The Milky Way was seen as a waterway in the heavens, sailed upon by both the sun deity and the moon, leading the ancient Egyptians to describe it as The Nile in the Sky. Due to this, and the name mehturt, she was identified as responsible for the yearly inundation of the Nile. Another consequence of this name is that she was seen as a herald of imminent birth, as when the amniotic sac breaks and floods its waters, it is a medical indicator that the child is due to be born extremely soon. Another interpretation of the Milky Way was that it was the primal snake, Wadjet, the protector of Egypt who was closely associated with Hathor and other early deities among the various aspects of the great mother goddess, including Mut and Naunet. Hathor also was favoured as a protector in desert regions (see Serabit el-Khadim).

Hathor's identity as a cow, perhaps depicted as such on the Narmer Palette, meant that she became identified with another ancient cow-goddess of fertility, Bat. It still remains an unanswered question amongst Egyptologists as to why Bat survived as an independent goddess for so long. Bat was, in some respects, connected to the Ba, an aspect of the soul, and so Hathor gained an association with the afterlife. It was said that, with her motherly character, Hathor greeted the souls of the dead in Duat, and proffered them with refreshments of food and drink. She also was described sometimes as mistress of the necropolis. The assimilation of Bat, who was associated with the sistrum, a musical instrument, brought with it an association with music. In this later form, Hathor's cult became centred in Dendera in Upper Egypt and it was led by priestesses and priests who also were dancers, singers and other entertainers.

Crystalinks cite: http://www.crystalinks.com/hathor.html. "In Egyptian mythology, Hathor (Egyptian for House of Horus) was originally a personification of the Milky Way, which was seen as the milk that flowed from the udders of a heavenly cow.

Hathor was an ancient goddess, worshipped as a cow-deity from at least 2700 BC, during the 2nd dynasty, and possibly even by the Scorpion King.

The name Hathor refers to the encirclement by her, in the form of the Milky Way, of the night sky and consequently of the god of the sky, Horus.

She was originally seen as the daughter of Ra, the creator whose own cosmic birth was formalised as the Ogdoad cosmogeny. An alternate name for her, which persisted for 3,000 years, was Mehturt (also spelt Mehurt, Mehet-Weret, and Mehet-uret), meaning great flood, a direct reference to her being the milky way.

The Milky Way was seen as a waterway in the heavens, sailed upon by both the sun god and the king, leading the Egyptians to describe it as The Nile in the Sky.

Due to this, and the name mehturt, she was identified as responsible for the yearly inundation of the Nile."

MYSTICAL LOTUS SEQUENCE

The mystical sequence goes like this. The virgin girl appears upon the great wheel of the lesser zodiac. She is the house of the cosmic twelve signs. At the thirteenth sign, the hidden door becomes open or fertile. The female fluids of life flow through her. They are represented by the opening lotus flower. She is three phases of woman in one. She is the pre-sexual little girl. She is the mate of the fertile male one – the woman. She is that which is called mother. The lotus that she so fondly plays with is like the fairy's wand. The touch of it can bring forth great pleasure. The touch of it can bring forth great pain. It is a star wand. It is the lotus; a pistol with the leaves wrapped around the stem. This allows the drop of cosmic dew to collect as its nectar. The wand, so to speak, is like the adze tool. This tool is half of the device used in The Book of Life to open the hood of Ra. Ra is the man whom when standing erect with outstretched arms and legs together appears as the key of life – the ankh. The two, the adze tool, which fits inside of the mystical ankh symbol which can be inserted into the male's mouth to manually perform the ritual called opening the hood of Ra.

The ankh and the adze tool make up the great fish hook of the fishers of men. This is not a net, but a type of hook like the symbolic English letters j, f, r, c, I, g, k, l, m, n, q, s, t, u, v, x, and y. Some are capital letters while others are lower case. In fishing the cosmic zodiac, the reel cord attaches to the letters at different points. This is why if you study ancient letter forms, sometimes the letters are turned at different angles. So here we have some of the different type of fishing hooks. The woman, as I said, is really three women in one. In her virgin state, she is the unknown object of his desire. <I cannot help myself: "She is the freak of his desire. When she dances, she sets your pants on fire. She is the freak of the <cosmic cycle> week!" George Clinton/Parliament Funkadelic.> In her union state with man, she becomes his dwelling place. She is like his mystical cave. <"She was not just knee deep, she was totally deep when she did "the freak" with me" - George Clinton>. From the mystical union <The Love Vibration – Bootsy Collins>; <Called The Cosmic Slop – George Clinton>, comes forth a baby <Star Child – George Clinton>. This is the point where the male's perception should begin to change. His eyes should start to open <"My God, what have I done?" Talking Heads: Once in a Life Time>.

Now, the woman is a dual creature. She is "wife" to one, while mother to another from the one. In the natural order, she breast feeds the baby. The man, having been a baby might be able to remember the feeding process. In general, the baby pacifier looks like the symbolic ankh. The nipple of the pacifier fits right at the bolt of "brahma nadi". <Look, there is a man on stage playing music sucking on a baby pacifier. It is a full grown man with a diaper on. He represents the three stages of life for men. In stage one, he is a baby. In stage two, he is aware of nocturnal emissions. In stage three, he has bladder control problems are said to be caused by the changing's of his emotions. The nocturnal emissions let him know that his sexual system is ready to fire. But, what is his response to this occurrence if he never heard about it? Did he break his insides, internal obelisk, or Osirius' column? And, who was that woman? She was Kundian, the woman of his dreams. She was Kundian, the guardian of his seed. She was Kundian, the nasty, vicious, jealous, spiteful, torturous, did I say hateful, woman of his nightmares. She, Kundian, is the jilted inner woman of man called his first love. Her energy is what caused the man to become the male that he is. Kundians perspective is: "How could you love her when I loved you first?" Kundian becomes somewhat annoyed at the seed that she guards being spent on another female. But because she is as a cosmic mother, she takes joy in the baby coming forth. In a way, it is her baby also because she provided the cosmic force that intertwined with the ejaculation.

But, let things go wrong between mommy and daddy! Kundian becomes the living nightmare of "I told you so"! Kundian chases the male's ass all around the zodiac. Kundian, whom at the beginning of the great journey, was like the happy Sphinx. Now she shows her teeth and wings to chase the man all around The Great Pyramid. Kundian wants to devour his ass. The man was so smart. The man could answer the mystical question to go inside of the pyramid into the mystical middle/queen's conception chamber of another woman. Now, Kundian, the mystical mythological beast witch demon is chasing the man's ass all up, down, and around The Great Pyramid. It is like the shell game, but the man cannot hide in the smaller pyramids. The two represent the breast of the woman. One the man knew, the other the baby <of man> knew. Kundian is very angry about the spent seed of man. There is only one place for man to hide. Man must hide in the dark in the temple of the three chambers called The Great Pyramid. Poor man, if he fails, he can slide down to the lowest chamber called The Pit. Poor man, if he did so so, he can dwell in the void of the Queen's Chamber. Poor man; if he can overcome, he can regenerate using the mystical coffer. You have to understand that the pyramid play is spiritual in symbolic in nature. So the poor man moves about inside the pyramid. The shafts point to stars which could be called cosmic lights. The poor man would like to go to "a" light, but Kundian, the beast, is waiting for him. It is as if she is standing on one paw <the same one she used to cover the mystical amphora, I had once seen an image where The Sphinx had its paw over an open jar with a wheel in it> atop of the pyramid, juggling the search lights of the Sun and Moon with two paws. The third paw is used to rotate the pyramid, hence the earth Kundian is watching like a never sleeping cat. Sometimes she has one eye open while the other is closed. Always on her face that silly ass full smile grin. Kundian is going to get you. Her objective is to drain the cosmic energy off of man's seed. She is going to dissipate your internal battery. I say this because it has been implied before: "Kundian is "a _ _ _ _ _ _"! Naw, naw, naw; I will tell you why this has been said about her in a minute.

When the aging man starts to realize that he is losing his vital power, that is when his perspective on life might change. He might then begin to ponder on the/his "meaning of life". His attitude towards the world might change. In reflection, he might think of that stupid question of the Sphinx. "What goes on all fours in the morning, by two in the mid day, and by three in the afternoon?" It is man. It is the baby, middle age, and elder man. So here is our hero wanting to help himself. This takes time from the female Kundian. He starts to perform yoga and tries to eat better. This is very irritating to Kundian. The man begins to study on now to build his Chang. Oh, Chang is his vital essence. He tries to reason with Kundian about the situation. They are not going to have any more children. What is the big deal? This drives Kundian wild on the earth plane.

Back to our story. Our friend, the hero, is trapped in The Great Pyramid. This is the Biblical equivalent of facing the symbolic meaning of the cross, proceeded spiritual danger, then making a run for sanctuary inside of the sacred temple. He can't stay there forever. He is in the room called The Queen's Chamber waiting for his heart to be weighed against a feather. This will decide if he ascends or descends. He can be tested or face the Sphinx "sitting by the door". He decides to get tested. And so, he ascends into the sarcophagus in The King's Chamber. He is lying inside of a stone box inside of what could be called the cosmic earth egg. On the bottom of the coffer lid are secret instructions. They were left by "The Hidden Master". Now because our friend, the hero had been working on his Chang; he had an option other than to face Kundian that day. He would spiritually travel back and forth between the two chambers. He still did his special exercises to increase his special "Chang" powers. He kept looking towards the dark sky for a sign. He knew his chakras were related to the lesser zodiac. If he was reading the secret tablet correctly, he could align the seven chakras to make a conjunction. A Bright light like the now talked about conjunction of Jupiter, Saturn, and The Earth in 7 B.C. The odds of him being able to do such a thing if we use the whole Tree of Life model of ten spheres making seven levels would be:

1) 360
2) 12,600
3) 46656000
4) 1679616000
5) 6046617600000
6) 217678233600000
7) 7836416409600000
8) 282110990745600000
9) 1.01559556668416e+23
10) 3.656158440062976e+25 odds to one. That is not bad.

Here we have our friend, the man, stuck inside of "the temple of knowledge" called The Great Pyramid. In contemplating the options, he looks upon the greater and lesser wheels of the zodiac for help. He then began to try to think like the Egyptians. He decided to wait until the lesser and greater zodiacs were in alignment. He would make his move in the sign of Gemini The Twins. He knows that the great mythological Sphinx is waiting for him to try to breach the gates. He chooses the twin sign of Gemini as his point of approach. In this, it is an active form of yin and yang. Having said that, the yin and yang signs can be viewed as the motion of two mystical dragons. These two dragons' interactions cause a third dynamic force. In the Kundalini Science, the two dragons are Ida and Pangala. They interface with each other in the "root chakra". The result of this action causes an energy winding cortex seepage that is called Kundalini energy. This Kundalini energy ascends and descends the central path of the euthric Tree of Life like the Hebrew Flame Letter "Daleth"! If you cipher the term Daleth, you could come up with "the lad". Who is the lad? He is the one upon the path of life whom is called "The Fool" in the Tarot language. In choosing the sign of the twins, our friend, the man, determines that "the ascending and descending path/paths" symbolically mimic the yin and yang signs inside of The I-Ching.

In the moment, the man makes the decision to take on the false form of the happy mythological dragon. This would give him abilities similar to that of The Sphinx. To this, the man can add the knowledge of The Great Pyramid to his arsenal. When all of this is done, the man is ready for the grand opening or metamorphous <Strong's Concordance number Greek: 3339> of light. This is sometimes called The Rebirth. You can think of it as the caterpillar changing into a butterfly. The butterfly is the "new form" that takes the path of ascension. The moth is the "new form" that takes the path towards the pit <this comes from Strong's Concordance numbers: Greek 3326 and 3445 in reference to Mathew 17:2 and Mark 9:2>.

So The Great Pyramid of Knowledge now becomes the cocoon of transformation. Upon the moment of the transformation, light breaks forth from inside of The Great Pyramid. The outer stones begin to vibrate loudly. This light eclipses the Sun light. Suddenly, the pyramid crystal shatters with an awful sound. Off comes the mythical 144,000 limestone polished white casing stones. The pyramid opens as it was built from "the top down". Of course, the pyramid is built from the ground up. This saying implies that The Great Pyramid is designed by the stars above. The massive disbursement of light solidifies the Kundalini statue guard called The Sphinx. The Sphinx has returned to its base or plateau. The "Great Work" is done.

There is more that I would like to tell you. I hope to publish more. In the mean time, I suggest you go down to The Harlem Park Community Baptist Church at 614 N. Gilmor Street Baltimore, Maryland 21217-2101. Hopefully, Reverend Kelly can help you to a basic level to get your mind right.

TIME LINE

As I leave from my concentrated effort to understand the message that the Egyptian culture was trying to leave to man, I wanted to reflect upon a few points. There is a major four set of books called *Pyramidology* by Adam Rutherford. This is an outstanding research document that I would say is of the highest order. This set of books is what I would call incredible. The one complaint that I have about the set is that it lists five books. From what I can find, the fifth book was never published. In this book, a time line was given. The book lists the year 1914 as a key year. The books states the date is pointed to by the use of something called a "pyramid inch". The book talks about this secret measurement. The year 1914 is said to point out the year of some special event. The book explains a revelation that the date of 1914 is predicted thousands of years ago. I feel that this particular document set will be very helpful to the religious community. My first comment relates to the book set itself. In the year 1914, it is said that World War I started. I imagine that Mr. Rutherford must have felt very strange. I say this for two reasons. The first reason is because Mr. Rutherford was saying that this major war event had been predicted thousands of years before in a part of a large document of prophecy built into stone. What might have Mr. Rutherford been thinking about this possible reality? On one hand, there may be a group of people that are causing these events to happen. On the other hand, the reality of the possible truth of the message would be "spooky" to say the least. I had at one time coined the term "spiritual shock"! I feel that Mr. Rutherford would have come across this level of awareness.

Now, here is what I found to be weird about the work of Mr. Rutherford and the stated date in question. The first thing is that there is a fifth missing book. The book that I found and used as key relating to the Book of the Revelation was written in 1914. I found that to be strange. I said to myself, "Hey, the cipher key text was written that year!" Wow, that sure was strange. What a prize! Would you agree if you had found an almost hundred year old cipher key to the Book of The Revelation? What would you do? Would you just marvel at it? Would you read it? If it gave you an answer, would you listen and move forward; or would you be satisfied just to have found it? Suppose you could not understand what you found? Would you study further, or would you just lay back? Maybe the game is a foot so to speak! Would you change your life patterns to pursue "the path", or would you just stay the course of your comfortable ego? These are just a few of the questions that needed to be answered.

So you found a hidden "lost" prize that you cannot even understand. What would you do? Would you research, or would you just stop to say "here it is"? Here is the strange part. The text is written by someone named "prize". I would like to spell a word for you. The word is "pryse". How do you feel about those two words? One is a type of reward. The other is the last name of the author of The New Testament cipher. His name is James Morgan Pryse. The book is called *The Restored New Testament*, How strange is that? So, now I have stated for you two books or keys. I hope I had mentioned The Blazing Star and the Jewish Kabbalah by William B. Green, ISBN 0-9254-086-9. Of course, there is The Sphinx Mystery by Robert Temple, ISBN 978-159477271-9. Yes, the Sphinx looks like it has a re-carved head. That relates to the training of the ignorant "beast" thinking type of human to that which has learned the knowledge and been transformed mentally into the biblical image of their makers' mindset. I could put it like this; the Sphinx symbolically represents the knowledge mindset of god man and man beast. To put that another way, the Sphinx is a symbolic representation of having knowledge of Good and Evil! I hope that this is enough to hold you! I just cannot leave out the master work by John White, Kundalini, Evolution and Enlightenment. This is a concentrated effort to decipher "what has been written" about the kundalini science. That is not to say that I think the author has firsthand knowledge of the science because I found several things missing. That is just my opinion.

There is one other book that I would like to mention. It deals with 'who" built The Great Pyramid at Giza? Who is the deceptive leading question of the question? How is the question? Joseph Davidovits gave the answer as being "concrete". But it would take a very long time to dry! Not if you saw the film I did on the Hover Dam. The film suggests that super concrete structures must be built in cells. Using that theory, I could see how you could build a concrete pyramid with the aid of a checker/chess board. Maybe many toys are not just toys! I hope that I have given enough. I know that I did my best.

> Malachi 3:16 – Then they that feared the LORD spake often one to another; and the LORD harkened, and heard [if], and a book of remembrance was written before him for them that feared the LORD, and that thought upon his name. If any man has an ear, let him hear.

cite: http://www.blueletterbible.org
I hope to see you on the web at www.unseenbooks.com, but now I have given "you" my keys! Whatever?

Frank M. Conaway, Jr.
Pen Name
META 3.14
3/26/11

REAR COVER

In this document, I discuss a theory that certain evidence about The Great Pyramid of Giza points to. The real conclusion was come to by using some theories as pointed to by the use of sacred geometry. This specialized science deals with pi, phi, e, the square root of negative one, ratios in the structure, Hebrew gematria, kabbalah, tarot arcana, and the Pythagorean theorem. Fibonacci sequences a.k.a. Leonardo of Pisa, Platonic solids, <come on, I know – some of them that I know want to "play" with me – so come on>, and a very strange "prophecy" time line said to exist in the grand gallery of The Great Pyramid. I also offer two possible additions to that time line. I offer to you a few very hidden texts that I feel are very important to them whom are on the great quest for knowledge. I hope that this will be helpful to you whom are interested.

REAR COVER

In 2004 I ciphered "Eternal Egypt" which was produced by the British Museum. The text on page 28 reads: "there are two significant barriers to our engagement with Egyptian art. The first barrier is inadequate knowledge. Even among scholars, this ignorance encompasses not only basic questions about the dates of some of the works, but also larger and more persuasive uncertainties about meaning, purpose, and function. We do know that almost all Egyptian art was in some sense religious." I could have ciphered it in 2001 when I recorded Baptist Gnostic Christian Eubonic Kundalinion Spiritual Ki Do Hermeneutic Metaphysics ISBN # 0-595-20678-6. On October 23, 2009 the show "Sex in the Ancient World – Egypt" aired on The History Channel. In the show, it was stated that: "the images contain a code", "what we do know is that 3,000 years later, experts regard it as one of the most important artifacts of antiquity." The show was advertised as the first public unveiling in 30 years after it was found and hidden by the Egyptologist. They still don't know what it means after 30 hidden years trying to decipher it. I offer you the ciphered answer to Revelation 13:18 and The Turin Erotic Papyrus Stela 55001.

BY FRANK M. CONAWAY JR.

REAR COVER 2

For centuries Christians have searched for the answer to Revelation 13:18 of The Bible. I found several answers to the question. I found one answer with a cipher key to the rest of the text. Even with the key, it was hard to understand what was to be done. It could be called The Great Work.

www.ingramcontent.com/pod-product-compliance
Lightning Source LLC
Chambersburg PA
CBHW032042150426
43194CB00006B/395

* 9 7 8 0 5 7 8 1 0 0 7 9 1 *